INSIGHT GUIDES

LONDON
StepbyStep

Discovery
CHANNEL

APA PUBLICATIONS L
Part of the Langenscheidt Publishing Group

CONTENTS

Introduction
About this Book   4
Recommended Tours   6

Orientation
Overview   10
Food and Drink   14
Shopping   18
History: Key Dates   20

Walks and Tours
1. The Big Sights   24
2. National Galleries   31
3. Covent Garden
   and Soho   34

4. Piccadilly and
   Mayfair   40
5. Marylebone   44
6. Regent's Park   46
7. Bloomsbury   48
8. Holborn   52
9. The City   55
10. South Bank   60
11. Tate to Tate   68
12. Hyde Park   72
13. South Kensington
   and Knightsbridge 76
14. Chelsea   81
15. Routemaster
   Bus Trip   84

16. Hampstead   86
17. Notting Hill   88
18. The East End   90
19. Greenwich   94
20. Kew   98

Directory
A–Z of Practical
   Information   102
Accommodation   112
Restaurants   118

Credits and Index
Picture Credits   124
Index   125

ABOUT THIS BOOK

This *Step by Step Guide* has been produced by the editors of Insight Guides, whose books have set the standard for visual travel guides since 1970. With top-quality photography and authoritative recommendations, this guidebook brings you the very best of London in a series of 20 tailor-made tours.

WALKS AND TOURS

The walks and tours in this book are designed to provide something to suit all budgets, tastes and trip lengths. As well as covering London's many attractions, the tours track numerous lesser-known sights and up-and-coming areas; there are also excursions for those who want to extend their visit outside the city.

The tours embrace a range of interests, so whether you are an art fan, an architecture buff, a gourmet, a lover of flora and fauna, a royalist or have children to entertain, you will find an option to suit. There are even options that will keep you as dry as possible if it rains.

We recommend that you read the whole of a tour before setting out. This should help you to familiarise yourself with the route and enable you to plan where to stop for refreshments – options for this are shown in the 'Food and Drink' boxes, recognisable by the knife and fork sign, on most pages.

For our pick of the walks by theme, consult Recommended Tours For… *(see pp.6–7)*.

ORIENTATION

The tours are set in context by this introductory section, giving an overview of the city to set the scene, plus background information on food and drink and shopping. A succinct history timeline in this chapter highlights the key events that have shaped London over the centuries.

DIRECTORY

Also supporting the tours is the Directory chapter, comprising a user-friendly, clearly organised A–Z of practical information, our pick of where to stay while you are in the city and select restaurant listings; these eateries complement the more everyday cafés and restaurants that feature within the tours themselves and are intended to offer a wider choice for evening dining.

Above from top: Whitehall street sign; cosmopolitan traders at Borough Market; the London Review Bookshop, near the British Museum; the bold gate at the British Library; taking a break in Regent's Park.

The Author

Michael Macaroon is a writer specialising in travel and the arts. He lives in London and finds the city rather like marmite: concentrated, intense, inimitable and, once your taste for it has developed, decidedly moreish. Macaroon's favourite restaurant in London is either Beigel Bake on Brick Lane or L'Artiste Musclé on Shepherd Market; his latest pub choice is the Mitre, an historic watering hole just off Hatton Garden. Macaroon is also the author of Insight's *Smart Guide Paris* and *Step by Step Paris*.

Margin Tips

Shopping tips, quirky anecdotes, historical facts and interesting snippets help visitors to make the most of their time in the city.

Feature Boxes

Notable topics are highlighted in these special boxes.

Key Facts Box

This box gives details of the distance covered on the tour, plus an estimate of how long it should take. It also states where the route starts and finishes, and gives key travel information such as which days are best to do the tour or handy transport tips.

Route Map

Detailed cartography shows the itinerary clearly plotted with numbered dots. For more detailed mapping, see the pull-out map slotted inside the back cover.

Food and Drink

Recommendations of where to stop for refreshment are given in these boxes. The numbers prior to each café/restaurant name link to references in the main text. Places recommended en route are also plotted on the maps.

The £ signs given in each entry reflect the approximate cost of a two-course meal for one, with half a bottle of house wine. These should be seen as a guide only. Price ranges, which are also quoted on the inside back flap for easy reference, are as follows:

££££	£40 and above
£££	£25–40
££	£15–25
£	£15 and below

Footers

The footers on left-hand pages give the itinerary name, plus, where relevant, a map reference; those on the right-hand pages cite the main attraction on the double page.

ARCHITECTURE

The Big Sights (walk 1) covers the architecture of royalty and government, the City (walk 9) contrasts Wren churches with steel-and-glass showpieces, and Greenwich (walk 19) is home to well-preserved Queen Anne and Georgian elegance.

RECOMMENDED TOURS FOR...

ART BUFFS

There's something for every palette, from the world-class National Gallery (walk 2) and Tate Modern (walk 11) to the best of British at the National Portrait Gallery (walk 2) and Tate Britain (walk 11), from elite Mayfair galleries (walk 4) to contemporary art in Hoxton (walk 18).

COOL BRITANNIA

Find the cutting edge in Soho's bars and clubs (walk 3) and the boho markets of Portobello Road (walk 17) and the fashionable East End (walk 18). For Brit Art, visit Tate Britain (tour 11).

FAMILIES WITH KIDS

For those who won't grow up there's lots to appeal, such as London Zoo (walk 6), dinosaurs at the Natural History Museum (walk 13), hands-on fun at the Science Museum (walk 13) and a London bus ride (route 15).

FLORA

London has more green spaces than any comparable city and many opportunities for a fix of flora. Regent's Park has fine rose gardens (walk 6), Kew is renowned for its royal botanic gardens (tour 20), but don't overlook Chelsea's Physic Garden (walk 14).

FOOD AND DRINK

The biggest choice of restaurants is in the West End, from Soho's Chinatown to Covent Garden's good-value pre-theatre suppers (walk 3). For fresh, organic produce visit Borough Market on the South Bank (walk 10) and for ethnic cuisine head to the East End (walk 18).

LITERARY LONDON

'When a man is tired of London, he is tired of life', quoth Dr Johnson. Head to Holborn (walk 8) and Bloomsbury (walk 7) to follow in his footsteps as well as those of Charles Dickens and Virginia Woolf; poetic sensibilities should visit Hampstead (walk 16), home of Keats.

RAINY DAYS

Sit it out in the larger London institutions such as the National Galleries (walk 2), the British Museum (walk 7), the Tate galleries (tour 11) or the South Kensington museums (walk 13). Alternatively, take a ride on a classic Routemaster bus (tour 15) past St Paul's cathedral and other City landmarks.

ROYAL LONDON

Have a royal time visiting London's big sights, such as Buckingham Palace, Changing the Guard and Clarence House (walk 1). Kensington Palace and the Albert and Princess Diana memorials are found in Hyde Park (walk 12).

SHOPPERS

Shop exhaustively on Oxford Street (walk 4), fashionably in Covent Garden (walk 3), exclusively in Mayfair (walk 4), smartly in Chelsea (walk 14) and alternatively in Notting Hill (walk 17).

SERVICE AREA
Please keep clear

ORIENTATION

An overview of London's geography, customs and culture, plus illuminating background information on food and drink, shopping and history.

CITY OVERVIEW   10

FOOD AND DRINK   14

SHOPPING   18

HISTORY: KEY DATES   20

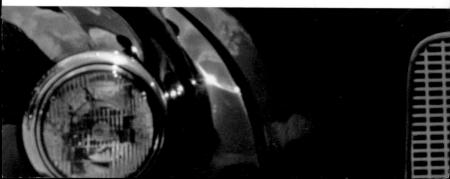

INTRODUCTION

Fire, plague, population explosions, aerial bombing, economic recessions, urban blight, terrorism… London has taken everything history could throw at it, and this has made it one of the world's most complex and fascinating cities.

Mother Tongue
A recent survey found that more than 300 languages (from Akan to Zulu) are spoken by London's school-children. After English, the most widely spoken are Bengali and Sylheti, Panjabi, Gujarati, and Hindi/Urdu.

Below: parliament and Whitehall.

There must be something special about London to attract more than 27 million overnight visitors each year. And it is not the weather. There are, however, wonderful palaces and cathedrals, theatres and museums, parks and gardens, restaurants serving cuisine from all parts of the world, a thriving nightlife, and a refreshingly cosmopolitan and open attitude towards diversity in all things, especially its own inhabitants.

POPULATION

Population Growth

The population of London currently stands at over 7.5 million people and is forecast to grow to over 8 million by 2016. London is generally considered the most populous city and metropolitan area in the European Union (EU). Of course, there are questions over where the boundaries of London's sprawl lie, but the city is usually held to constitute the 32 administrative boroughs of 'Greater London'.

The population on this territory rose from about 1.1 million in 1801 to peak at over 8.6 million in 1939. It then declined to 6.7 million in 1988, before growing once more to about the same level today as in 1970 (also the level of the 1920s). However, the wider metropolitan area of London continues to spread outwards and is now home to between 12 and 14 million, depending on the definition of that area.

Ethnicity

More than one in three London residents are from a minority ethnic group. Figures from the Office for National Statistics show that, as of 2006, London's foreign-born population is 2.3 million (31 per cent), up from 1.6 million in 1997. Of this

number, about 39 per cent are from the Indian sub-continent and about 35 per cent are African or Afro-Caribbean. In addition, there has recently been an influx of hundreds of thousands of workers from the new member countries of the EU, particularly Poland.

Of course, London has been a focus of immigration for centuries, whether as a place of safety (as with the Huguenots fleeing Catholic France, or Eastern European Jews escaping Nazism) or for economic reasons (as with the Irish, Bangladeshis and West Indians).

Wealth Distribution

London ranks as one of the most expensive cities in the world, alongside Tokyo and Moscow. At one end of the scale, London is ranked 4th in the world in number of billionaire residents. There is also the City of London, renowned for awarding stellar bonuses to its star employees.

At the other end of the scale are the down-and-outs sleeping rough in shop doorways and newly arrived economic immigrants who are living in cramped boarding houses. In the past, the East End has hosted numerous impoverished arrivals from overseas. Many have subsequently moved elsewhere in London as they have gained prosperity. A higher percentage of Indians and Pakistanis, for example, now own their own homes in the capital than white people.

Above from far left: Millennium Bridge and St Paul's; Coldstream Guard at the Changing the Guard ceremony outside Buckingham Palace; the London Eye; taxi at night.

London Cabbies

About 20,000 drivers work in London, half of them as owner-drivers. The others either hire vehicles from big fleets or work night shifts in someone else's cab. Would-be drivers must register with the Public Carriage Office and then spend up to four years learning London in minute detail – known as 'the Knowledge'. They achieve this by travelling the streets of the metropolis on a moped, whatever the weather, working out a multitude of routes from a clipboard mounted on the handlebars. So even if the supposedly garrulous cabbies do not always know what they are talking about, they do know where they are going. The classic cab itself – or Hackney Carriage, as it is officially known – is the FX4, launched in 1959, and still going strong in its updated incarnation (with full wheelchair access). The traditional manner for hailing a cab is to raise your furled brolly and shout, 'Taxi!' The cab may not always stop though: Prince Philip and the comedian Stephen Fry are known to maintain their own black cabs, so that they can travel around the city in anonymity.

Sport in London The 2012 Olympics will be hosted by London, with much of the games taking place in Stratford in East London, which is undergoing major regeneration as a result. If your visit to the capital does not coincide with this event, there is still plenty on offer: world-class football at Arsenal and Chelsea; cricket at Lord's and the Oval; tennis at Wimbledon; horse-racing a short train ride away at Ascot; rugby at Twickenham; boxing at Bethnal Green's York Hall; and greyhound racing, at Walthamstow.

THE CLIMATE

London has a mild climate. Snow (other than a light dusting) and temperatures below freezing are fairly unusual, with January temperatures averaging 6°C (43°F). In the summer months, temperatures average 18°C (64°F), but can rise much higher, causing the city to become stiflingly hot (air-conditioning is not universal). Heat stored by the city's buildings creates a microclimate with temperatures up to 5 °C (9 °F) warmer in the city than in the surrounding areas. Even so, summer temperatures rarely rise much above 33 °C (91.4 °F), and the highest temperature ever recorded in London was 38.1 °C (100.6 °F), measured at Kew Gardens during the European heat wave of 2003.

Day to day fluctuations can be significant, though, and surprise showers catch people unprepared all year round. This enables the populace to engage in a favourite topic of conversation and tut-tut over inclement spells. Whatever the season, visitors should come prepared with wet-weather clothes (traditionally a mackintosh or storm cape and sou' wester) and other useful apparatus (umbrella, headscarf, tweed hat, etc.).

LONDON GEOGRAPHY

The Political Map

When people talk about London, they are usually referring to the area covered by Greater London. This administrative organisation was imposed on the city in 1965. It comprises the City of London and 32 London boroughs.

Originally, there were two cities here: the City of Westminster (centred on the Houses of Parliament and Westminster Abbey) and the City of London (often referred to simply as 'the City', and covering what is now the financial district – the historic square mile between St Paul's Cathedral and the Tower of London). Westminster is now a borough just like any other, governed by a borough council. The City of London, on the other hand, has its own unique institutions of local government dating back to the 12th century: the Corporation of London, headed by the Lord Mayor.

Presiding over Greater London at the top level is the Greater London Authority (GLA) with, at its head, a directly elected mayor (not to be confused with the Lord Mayor of the City of London). The Mayor and the GLA are responsible for the Metropolitan Police Authority, the London Fire and Emergency Planning Authority, the London Development Agency and Transport for London. Local services such as refuse disposal, housing grants and parking control are still run by the 32 boroughs.

North–South, East–West

Whatever the political subdivisions of London, the physical and social ones are often more significant. Not least of these is the river Thames, dividing the city into north and south. London north of the river has historically been the location of government and commerce. The south, apart from the river

Above black cab; blue plaque.

Frost Fairs

Between 1400 and 1900 there were 23 winters in which the river Thames froze over at London. When the ice was thick enough and lasted long enough, festivals were held on the river, featuring everything from skating to bull-baiting to horse races, and even, at the last frost fair, in 1814, an elephant, led across below Blackfriars Bridge. The river has not frozen over since then: the climate has grown milder, old London Bridge (which had slowed up the river flow) was demolished in 1831, and the river has been embanked, making it deeper and less liable to freezing.

banks themselves, was less developed until the 19th century, when it became a vast residential suburb. South London is still much less of a destination for a day out than north London, and cab drivers, notoriously, sometimes refuse to take you south of the river.

West London, especially Mayfair, Kensington and Chelsea, is the posh end of town. It is now particularly popular with wealthy foreign residents, attracted by the relative security of the area, the investment potential of owning one of its smart properties, and Britain's lenient tax regime. East London, on the other hand, has historically harboured some of the poorest communities in the city, with the indigenous working classes, close by London's docks, living alongside newly arrived immigrants. Parts of it are now far more vibrant than west London, popular with artists and a younger, more outward-looking generation.

HEAVEN AND HELL

The 18th-century man of letters, Samuel Johnson, famously declared, 'when a man is tired of London, he is tired of life; for there is in London all that life can afford.' This is still the case today: London offers some the chance to accumulate great wealth, others to be at the centre of cultural ferment, and many others the opportunity simply to be themselves in a tolerant and civilised environment (no matter what their creed or colour, sexual orientation or chosen lifestyle).

However, at times, London has

seemed less than idyllic. In 1819, the poet Shelley wrote, 'Hell is a city much like London/A populous and smoky city.' Indeed, at one time, the streets in the old City were so dark and narrow that shopkeepers had to erect mirrors outside their windows to reflect light into the shops. And pollution and congestion are still problems today, warranting the city's widely used nickname, 'The Big Smoke'.

The last 25 years, though, have seen something of a renaissance for the city, with the regeneration of neglected areas, a vibrant art and music scene, fuller employment, and even some improvements in public transport. This atmosphere of optimism and confidence reached its apogee in the late 90s, when London was the centre of what the media referred to as 'Cool Britannia', and was a magnet for many an aspiring mover and shaker.

FOOD AND DRINK

London's cuisine was once reputed to offer little more than overcooked stodge. Not so now: as well as impressive renditions of just about every other country's cuisine, you can appreciate the finest of Britain's own food heritage.

Above: knife, fork and napkin; decorative flowers; and coffee – all at Vinoteca *(see p.59).*

Top from left: bastion of traditional British dining, Simpson's in the Strand; Terence Conran's Bibendum, in the former Michelin tyre headquarters, Fulham Road; colourful bottles of olive oil; classic British fish and chips.

Opposite: bookish Asia de Cuba.

The last few decades have seen a remarkable transformation in London's restaurant scene, bringing it into the international league. Londoners' taste for innovative cooking of the best produce have made the city the envy of foreign capitals more traditionally regarded as gastronomically blessed. At one time, however, things were very different, and British food was the butt of many jokes, especially from the French. Jacques Chirac is quoted as saying that 'you can't trust people who cook as badly as that.' Nowadays, a good pork chop from St John or Scottish lobster at Gordon Ramsay would have him eating his words.

BRITISH CUISINE

As well as a great enthusiasm for foreign styles of cooking, the blossoming of London's restaurant scene is closely related to the re-evaluation of Britain's indigenous cuisine. A new generation of energetic head chefs has proved emphatically that British food is much more than meat and two veg, a stodgy pie full of gravy or a buttie stuffed with soggy chips. Now you can feast on Cromer crab, Cornish sprats, Gressingham duck, juicy Herdwick lamb, Galloway beef, and traditional desserts such as bread-and-butter pudding (deli-

ciously light when well prepared) or Eccles cakes with Lancashire cheese. And this new-found culinary zeal has also filtered down to the local pub, where potted shrimps, shepherd's pie, Lancashire hotpot and bangers and mash are cooked with care and served with pride.

PLACES TO EAT

High-End Restaurants

As well as long-established stalwarts such as Le Gavroche, in recent years London has nurtured numerous other Michelin-star contenders. Gordon Ramsay, Marcus Wareing, Tom Aikens, and Angela Hartnett among others have all raised expectations of what restaurants should be offering.

There are also influential establishments that more or less eschew the Michelin ethos. These include the River Cafe, with its unpretentious modern Italian cooking, and St John, which has spearheaded the renaissance of British cuisine. Both of these rely on high-quality produce to speak for itself with the minimum of fuss.

It is easily argued that many restaurants in London give too much emphasis to design and image and not enough to the food itself. At Sketch or China Tang for example, some feel

that if the food is fairly good, it is so as not to distract from the interior decoration. A step further are the likes of The Ivy or Cipriani, where it is the other diners, some of them celebrities, that are the focus of attention.

Many of the restaurants mentioned above require booking weeks, perhaps months, in advance. Beware also, if they take your credit card details when you book, you may be charged anyway if you do not then show up.

Pubs

If all this business of booking weeks ahead, hefty bills and embarrassing formality is more than you can take, do not fret; all is not lost. Many of the best eating experiences in London are quite inexpensive, relaxed affairs.

A major component of British social history is the public house, which in recent years has been re-evaluated. There is a lot to be said for a pie and a pint. For pub cuisine is a distinctive cuisine in itself (and that does not mean ploughman's lunch with a limp lettuce leaf and a wedge of cheese). Think of steak-and-kidney pudding, meat loaf, Lancashire hotpot, shepherd's pie, sausage and mash and the traditional Sunday roast. If well executed, these dishes can be delicious.

Many traditional pubs have now been converted into 'gastropubs', many sensitively, some crassly. The cliché is of a pub desecrated: its centuries-old patina stripped away, floorboards sanded down, walls painted white, shabby-chic furniture brought in and a blackboard advertising faux-Mediterranean dishes.

However, when it is done well, the gastropub can be very good. Try The Anchor and Hope on the South Bank, or The Coach and Horses on the edge of the City or The Cow on Westbourne Park Road near Notting Hill.

Ethnic Restaurants

Another mainstay of London's culinary heritage is the huge variety of ethnic restaurants, especially Indian, Chinese, Japanese, Vietnamese and Thai. According to the city authorities, 53 major country styles are represented among London's 6,000 licensed restaurants. Visit the Kingsland Road in the East End for Vietnamese, Whitechapel or Tooting (South London) for Indian, and Mayfair for (mostly upmarket) Japanese establishments.

Fish and Chips

Whereas in the 1930s there were more than 30,000, today there are only 8,600 fish-and-chip shops in Britain. The future of those remaining is threatened by dwindling fish stocks and fast-food corporations. In the past, cod was preferred in the south of Britain and haddock in the north. It is skate, however, which is the real test of a fryer's mettle: if it is cooked just right, it is soft and light, but, if only 90 per cent done, it is a glutinous, bony mess.

Beer Flood

In 1814, at a brewery on Tottenham Court Road, a huge vat containing over 135,000 gallons (511,000 litres) of beer ruptured, causing other vats in the same building to do the same, in a domino effect. More than 323,000 gallons (1,223,000 litres) of beer gushed into the streets. The tsunami of beer destroyed two homes and knocked down the wall of the Tavistock Arms pub, trapping the barmaid under the rubble. In all, nine people were killed: eight due to drowning, one from alcohol poisoning. The brewery was eventually taken to court over the accident, but the judge and jury ruled the disaster to be an 'Act of God'.

Greasy Spoons, Pie and Mash and Fish and Chips

Often overlooked is London's fast-disappearing old-fashioned working-class grub. Even 15 years ago, wherever you were in London, there was always a haven close at hand offering a plate of piping hot food at everyday prices. Now, the greasy spoon caffs, fish-and-chip, and pie-and-mash shops are being usurped by coffee bars and fast-food corporations who can pay grasping landlords' higher rents.

'Greasy spoon' cafes serve all-day breakfasts: eggs, bacon, chips and beans, sometimes with manly extras such as black pudding or bubble and squeak. Also, strong tea (in a mug on a saucer) and white bread and butter. Check out www.classiccafes.co.uk for an anthology of the best greasy spoon caffs still open.

Pie-and-mash shops serve meat pies or eels (jellied or stewed) with liquor (an odd sort of glop based on parsley sauce) and mashed potato. The premises themselves have wonderful tiled interiors, marble-topped tables and wooden benches. Good examples are M Manze's on Tower Bridge Road and F Cooke on Broadway Market in the East End.

Lastly come the fish-and-chip shops, with their fat stubby fried potatoes, quite impossible to replicate in a conventional kitchen, and fish in batter, double fried in beef dripping. Try Fryer's Delight in Holborn (see p. 52) and Rock and Sole Plaice in Covent Garden (see p.35).

Chains

London has ever more chain restaurants, more indeed than most other European cities. Some are reasonably good (Carluccio's or the Gourmet Burger Kitchen for example), others are hugely disappointing, with food microwaved from frozen, and staff as apathetic as you might expect on the minimum wage. Remarkably, it is sometimes the affluent areas (Hampstead, for example) that are the most intensive breeding ground for chains and have little else to offer besides.

DRINKS

Beer

Traditionally, beer was to Britain what wine was to France. It comes in various forms, from lager (now the most popular form in Britain) to ale (brewed using only top-fermenting yeasts; sweeter and fuller bodied) to stout (creamy, almost coffee-like beer made from roasted malts or roast barley), of which the most famous brand is probably Guinness.

Pubs generally serve beer either 'draught' or from the cask. In the case of the former, a keg is pressurised with carbon-dioxide gas, which drives the beer to the dispensing tap. For the latter, beer is pulled from the cask via a beer line with a hand pump at the bar. This method is generally used for what is often termed 'real ale': unfiltered and unpasteurised beer, which, unlike industrially produced lagers, requires careful storage at the correct temperature.

Wine

The popularity of wine-drinking in Britain has increased dramatically in

the last 20 years. In the unenlightened days, many pubs served only Liebfraumilch and perhaps Lambrusco, but nowadays you can expect a more grown-up selection, and New World wines are at least as widely offered by pubs as European wines. The growing popularity of wine in Britain has even encouraged some to start producing English varieties. Try the restaurant, Roast (see p.66), upstairs at Borough Market, for a good-quality selection of English wines.

Cider

A longer-established English tipple is cider, produced in south-west England since before the Romans arrived. Made from the fermented juice of apples, it is also known as 'scrumpy' (windfalls are 'scrumps'). The pear equivalent is called 'perry'. Unfortunately, many pubs only offer mass-produced cider made from apple concentrate. For the real thing, try The Blackfriar (see p.53), The Harp on Chandos Place, tucked just behind St-Martin-in-the-Fields (see p.25), or Chimes restaurant on Churton Street in Pimlico.

Whisky

Another speciality is whisky, produced in Scotland and Ireland. This is available as 'single malt' (malt whisky from a single distillery), as well as 'blended' – cheaper whiskies are normally made from a mixture of malt and grain whiskies from many distilleries. Most pubs in central London will offer a small selection of both, though aficionados may consider joining the

Whisky Society, which has its members' rooms above the Bleeding Heart Restaurant in Hatton Garden, Clerkenwell (Bleeding Heart Yard; tel: 020-7831 4447; www.smws.co.uk).

Last Orders

Most pubs ring a bell for 'last orders' at 11pm and then expect you to drink up and depart by 11.30pm. However, in 2003 new legislation was introduced allowing pub landlords to apply for extended opening hours, up to 24 hours a day, 7 days a week. In practice, only a small minority of pubs have made such an application, though this has not stopped renewed concern about Britain's supposed 'binge-drinking' culture.

Above from far left:
Raffles Brown's Hotel, a cosy setting for tea; profiteroles (left) and grilled fish (right), at St John Bread and Wine (see p.91); The Laughing Gravy.

Curry
A recent foreign secretary, Robin Cook, claimed that chicken tikka masala was 'Britain's true national dish'. Indeed, Britain's Indian restaurants now employ more people than her coal, steel and ship-building industries combined.

Food Markets

Perhaps the best of London's food markets for the visitor is Borough Market near London Bridge (Thur 11am–5pm, Fri noon–6pm, Sat 9am–4pm). It offers some of the country's best produce in an historic setting. For other farmers' markets, see www.lfm.org.uk. London's main wholesale markets are Smithfields for meat (Mon–Fri 4–10am), Billingsgate for fish (now in Docklands; offers some guided tours; Tue–Sat 5–8.30am) and Spitalfields for fruit and vegetables (now in Leyton; Mon–Fri midnight–1pm, Sat until 11am).

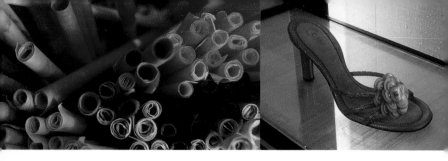

SHOPPING

Napoleon called England a nation of shopkeepers. Perhaps he had a point. Whether you are in the market for a grand piano or a custom-made brassiere, a pet parrot or a snuff box, there will be somewhere in London you can buy it.

Above: ready to wear; jeans at Top Shop, the world's largest fashion store; Jeremy Fisher at Peter Rabbit & Friends, Covent Garden.

Opening Hours
Most shops open from 9 or 10am until 6 or 6.30pm, with no break for lunch. West End shops usually open late on Thursday, until around 7 or 8pm. Many shops open on Sundays, although with shorter hours.

With over 30,000 shops, and everything available, from Old Masters to vintage film posters, and Savile Row suits to punk rock t-shirts, London is an easy place to spend your cash. And just to make it even easier, unlike in many other European capitals, Sundays and summer holidays are not sacred: this is a year-round shopper's destination.

SHOPPING AREAS

For those on a retail mission, the sheer size of the city means you have to be selective. However, London's shopping geography is relatively easy to navigate and can be loosely divided into shopping districts, each offering a distinctive experience. Indeed, in some cases there are whole streets devoted to one theme: Savile Row and Jermyn Street for gentlemen's outfitters, Hatton Garden for jewellery, Carnaby Street for branded street fashion.

The best means for getting from area to area is usually the tube, though for the journey home, those laiden with heavy bags may favour a taxi. The bus network has good coverage, but is slower and less easy to navigate. And of course, there is always a lot to be said for walking: distances between some streets – Oxford Street and Piccadilly, Regent Street and Bond Street – are short enough to walk.

Designer Districts
For those wanting the best of European and international designer fashions, Knightsbridge, home to the higher-end department stores Harrods and Harvey Nichols, has perhaps the highest concentration of such shops. Haute couture names from Armani to Yves Saint Laurent sit next to established British designers Katharine Hamnett, Anya Hindmarch and Bruce Oldfield, to name a few. Also out west are the King's Road and Fulham Road in Chelsea, with couturiers such as Hardy Amies and Amanda Wakeley sandwiched between smart interior design stores.

Bond Street, in Mayfair, also offers a vast choice of designer labels as well as the world's biggest names in jewellery, and some of London's top dealers in Old Masters and antique furniture. Cork Street, the next road along, is lined with dealers in modern art, while a little further east still is Savile Row *(see left)*.

Around Piccadilly
Around the Piccadilly area are some of London's oldest shops, many of which hold royal warrants to supply the Queen and her family with goods. On Piccadilly itself are upmarket grocer Fortnum & Mason and Hatchard's the booksellers. Parallel with Piccadilly is Jermyn Street, which specialises in

shirts, though it is also the place for the debonair to find that silk dressing gown or pair of monogrammed carpet slippers. On St James's, just nearby, is Lock's the hatters, and Lobb's the bootmakers. Then there is Regent Street, the world's first purpose-built shopping street, running north from Piccadilly Circus, and home to Britain's largest toy shop, Hamleys, as well as Liberty, the Arts-and-Crafts shopping institution.

Chains and Department Stores

High-street chains and department stores characterise Oxford Street, the capital's main shopping thoroughfare. Selfridges and John Lewis, near Bond Street tube, are perhaps the only destination shops here. Near Oxford Circus, running south, is Carnaby Street *(see left)*. Finally, at the eastern end of Oxford Street is Tottenham Court Road, dominated by electronics and hi-fi shops, as well as home furnishings stores, including Habitat and Heal's.

Soho and Covent Garden

Although Soho has never quite lost its seedy atmosphere, between the sex shops are some fine delicatessens as well as stores selling hip urbanwear. Bookworms should head for nearby Charing Cross Road (and Cecil Court too), with its second-hand bookshops and major branches of many of the large book chains.

Covent Garden offers high-street and urban fashion as well as specialist emporia dedicated to teapots or kites or cheese or wooden toys.

MARKETS

London has markets for antiques, crafts, clothes and, of course, food *(see p.17)*. For antiques enthusiasts, Portobello Road is the obvious choice, with the main market held on Saturdays. An alternative is Alfies Antique Market (Tue–Sat 10am–6pm) on Church Street near Marylebone. For a more upmarket affair, try the shops on Kensington Church Street, where more than 80 dealers display their finds.

For clothes and crafts, in the East End there are the weekend markets at Spitalfields and Brick Lane, as well as the week-day rag trade at Petticoat Lane (also Sun morning). Then there is Portobello Road (retro) and Camden Lock (retro, clubwear, goth and punk). At Greenwich market (Thur–Sun) the emphasis is on crafts and deli foods.

Above from far left: multicoloured paper at Papyrus; sexy shoes in upmarket Mayfair; dummies at Harrods; posh flowers on sale in South Kensington.

The Sales
There are two main sales periods across the UK – January, and July and August. Prices can be slashed by up to 50 per cent and more, especially on large items or last-season's fashions.

Below: Harrods Art Nouveau food hall.

HISTORY: KEY DATES

From humble beginnings, through sacking, fire, pestilence and war, and with renowned pomp and circumstance, London has grown to become one of the world's most culturally vibrant, cosmopolitan and ethnically diverse capitals.

EARLY PERIOD

AD 43	Emperor Claudius establishes the trade port of Londinium and builds a bridge over the river Thames.
61	Boudicca sacks the city but is defeated, and London is rebuilt.
c.200	City wall built. London is made the capital of Britannia Superior.
410	Romans withdraw to defend Rome. London falls into decline.
604	The first St Paul's Cathedral is founded by King Ethelbert.
c.750	The monastery of St Peter is founded on Thorney Island; it later becomes Westminster Abbey.
884	London becomes the capital under Alfred the Great.
1042	Edward the Confessor moves his court to Westminster.

AFTER THE CONQUEST

Above: Henry Fitzailwin, the first mayor of London; detail of The Globe from Visscher's map of London; Guy Fawkes and his fellow conspirators plot the destruction of the king, James I, and his parliament.

1066	William I, Duke of Normandy, conquers Britain.
1078	Tower of London's White Tower is built.
1191	London elects its first mayor, Henry Fitzailwin.
1348–9	Black Death wipes out about 50 per cent of London's population.
1534	Henry VIII declares himself head of the Church of England.
1558–1603	London is the capital of a mighty kingdom under Elizabeth I.
1599	The Globe theatre opens at Bankside.
1605	Guy Fawkes attempts to blow up James I and Parliament.
1642–9	Civil war between Cavalier Royalists and republican Roundheads. Royalists are defeated; Charles I is executed.
1660	The monarchy is restored under Charles II.
1664–6	Plague hits London again, killing around 110,000 citizens.
1666	Great Fire of London destroys 80 per cent of London's buildings.

AFTER THE FIRE

1675	Sir Christopher Wren begins to rebuild St Paul's Cathedral.
1764	The Literary Club is established by Samuel Johnson, compiler of the first English dictionary.

1783	Last execution held at Tyburn (Marble Arch).
1803–15	Napoleonic Wars .
1811–20	Prince Regent, later George IV: Regency style.
1824	Establishment of the National Gallery.
1834	Building starts on the Gothic-style Houses of Parliament still standing today after the old Palace of Westminster burns down.

THE AGE OF EMPIRE

1837–1901	Queen Victoria's reign, characterised by Empire-building and the Industrial Revolution.
1849	Tea merchant Henry Charles Harrod opens a shop in Knightsbridge.
1851	The hugely successful Great Exhibition is held in architect Joseph Paxton's Crystal Palace in Hyde Park.
1859	'Big Ben' bell is hung in the tower of the Palace of Westminster.
1863	London Underground opens its first line, the Metropolitan line.
1888	The serial murderer dubbed Jack the Ripper strikes in Whitechapel.

20TH CENTURY

1914–18	World War I. Zeppelins bomb London.
1922	British Broadcasting Company transmits its first radio programmes.
1939–45	World War II. London is heavily bombed, killing 29,000 people and damaging 80 per cent and destroying a third of buildings in the City.
1951	Festival of Britain. Southbank Centre built adjacent to Waterloo.
1960s	London christened the capital of hip for fashion, music and the arts.
1980s	Margaret Thatcher years. Several IRA bombs hit London.
1986	The Greater London Council is abolished by Thatcher.
1996	Shakespeare's Globe opens on Bankside.
1997	New Labour elected under Tony Blair. 'Cool Britannia' period.

21ST CENTURY

2000	Dome, London Eye, Tate Modern and Jubilee Line extension open to celebrate the millennium. Ken Livingstone elected mayor.
2001	Greater London Authority is re-established under Livingstone.
2003	A 'congestion charge' is introduced for traffic in central London.
2005	Labour are re-elected. London wins the bid for the 2012 Olympics. Terrorist bomb attacks on 7 July kill 52 and injure about 700.
2007	Gordon Brown succeeds Blair as prime minister.
2012	London hosts the Olympic Games.

Above from far left: historic depiction of the Thames, painted c.1822, by Robert Havell Jr.

Great Exhibition
In 1851 Queen Victoria (1837–1901) opened the Great Exhibition of the Works of all Nations in Hyde Park, its magnificent glass building – dubbed the 'Crystal Palace' – displaying Britain's skills and achievements to the entire world and attracting some 6 million visitors. With the profits of £186,000, Prince Albert (1819–61), Queen Victoria's German-born husband, realised his great ambition: a centre of learning. Temples to the arts and sciences blossomed in Kensington's gardens, nicknamed 'Albertopolis'. What was later named the Victoria and Albert Museum opened in 1857, followed by the Royal Albert Hall in 1871, the Albert Memorial in 1872 and then the Natural History Museum in 1881.

WALKS AND TOURS

1. The Big Sights   24

2. National Galleries   31

3. Covent Garden and Soho   34

4. Piccadilly and Mayfair   40

5. Marylebone   44

6. Regent's Park   46

7. Bloomsbury   48

8. Holborn and
    the Inns of Court   52

9. The City   55

10. The South Bank   60

11. Tate to Tate   68

12. Hyde Park   72

13. South Kensington
    and Knightsbridge   76

14. Chelsea   81

15. Routemaster Bus Trip   84

16. Hampstead   86

17. Notting Hill   88

18. The East End   90

19. Greenwich   94

20. Kew   98

THE BIG SIGHTS

In a changing world it's reassuring that Nelson's still on his column in Trafalgar Square, the prime minister's at no. 10 Downing Street, Big Ben is chiming at the Houses of Parliament and the Queen is at Buckingham Palace.

DISTANCE 3 miles (5km)
TIME A full day
START Trafalgar Square
END Buckingham Palace
POINTS TO NOTE

Changing the Guard in Whitehall is at 11am and at Buckingham Palace at 11.30am. A shorter version of this route could start at Trafalgar Square and then skip straight to the Mall section. In summer, last admission to Buckingham Palace is at 3.45pm.

This is the route to do if you are new to London or if you want to revisit the capital's major royal and political sights. Trafalgar Square, where this route begins, is very close to Charing Cross Station and Villiers Street, where we recommend a quick sharpener first at **Gordon's**, see ⑪①.

TRAFALGAR SQUARE

Trafalgar Square ❶ is plumb in the centre of London, as attested to by the plaque on the traffic island in the south

Above: Nelson's statue dominates Trafalgar Square; feeding the square's once-famous pigeons is now banned in order to bring their numbers down.

Christmas Tree
Every Christmas since 1947, the Norwegian government has presented a Norway Spruce to the people of London in gratitude for Britain's support during World War II. In the autumn, the Lord Mayor of Westminster visits Oslo to participate in the felling of the tree.

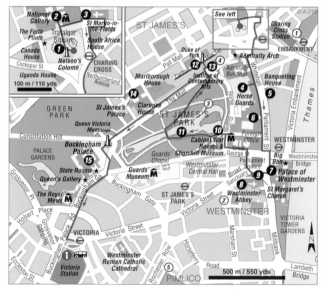

of the square. It was conceived by the Prince Regent in 1820, was designed in its current form by Sir Charles Barry in 1838, and assumed its current name in 1841 in commemoration of Nelson's victory over Napoleon's navy at the Battle of Trafalgar in 1805.

Nelson's Column

At the centre of the square is **Nelson's Column**, a 46-m (151-ft) granite pillar topped by an 18-ft (5.5-m) statue of Admiral Lord Nelson. Battle-scarred, with only one arm (though without a patch on his blind eye), he gazes south, surveying the fleet of miniature ships atop the flag poles lining the Mall. Completed in 1843, the column was designed by William Railton, and the statue by E.H. Baily. The four iconic lions at the base were added in 1867 by sculptor Edwin Landseer, who cast them from the metal of the cannons of the defeated French fleet.

Around the column are two fountains. Barry's originals were replaced with larger ones by Edwin Lutyens in 1939, allegedly to limit the square's capacity for political demonstrations. In the corners of the square are four plinths, with statues of General Charles Napier, Major General Sir Henry Havelock and George IV (astride a horse without a saddle, boots or stirrups); the fourth plinth was originally left empty but is now used to display works of contemporary art *(see right)*.

Bordering the Square

Around the square, Canada House, South Africa House and Uganda House are memories of distant Empire days. On the north side of the square is the **National Gallery ❷** *(covered in detail in walk 2)*, which displays pre-20th-century art. On the lawn in front is a statue of James II by Grinling Gibbons. Hand on hip, he is inexplicably dressed as an ancient Roman. Further along is a diminutive George Washington *(see p.2)*, a gift from the state of Virginia. He stands on soil imported from the US, honouring his declaration that he would never again set foot on British soil.

St Martin-in-the-Fields

On the east side of the square is the church of **St Martin-in-the-Fields ❸** (tel: 020-7766 1100; daily 8am–6pm; free). A church has stood on the site since the 13th century, when this area was fields between the City of Westminster and the City of London.

The present church was completed in 1726 to designs by James Gibbs. His amalgam of classical and baroque styles subsequently became the model for many churches in the US. The church was largely paid for by George III, and it remains Buckingham Palace's parish

The Fourth Plinth
Trafalgar Square's fourth plinth was left empty after plans in 1841 to erect an equestrian statue collapsed through lack of funds. Recent suggestions for a suitable occupant included Nelson Mandela, Princess Diana and David Beckham. Now, works of art are commissioned to take their turn, each for 18 months. At the time of writing, it was Thomas Schütte's *Model for a Hotel 2007*.

Food and Drink 🍴
① GORDON'S WINE BAR

47 Villiers Street; tel: 020-7930 1408; daily L and D, Mon–Fri B from 8am; ££
By Embankment tube, just behind Charing Cross, is this family-run bar. Quaff fine wines and scoff delicious pies and cheeses in the candlelit cellar of a building once inhabited by Samuel Pepys, and, much later, Rudyard Kipling. Seating outside in summer.

SOVEREIGN'S ENTRANCE

Above from left:
Scots Guard; royal
entrance at parliament.

Charles I Statue
Facing down Whitehall
from Trafalgar Square
is Hubert le Sueur's
statue of Charles I.
England's first
equestrian bronze,
it was cast in 1633,
then sold for scrap
during the Civil War
and only recovered
and set on its plinth
when the throne was
restored with the reign
of Charles II (1660–85).

War Monuments
In the middle of the
street outside the
Foreign Office stands
the Cenotaph, built by
Edwin Lutyens to
remember those who
died in World War I.
Nearby is a memorial
to the women of
World War II,
depicting sets of
women's work
clothes, hung up at
the end of the war.

church; the box to the left of the gallery
is reserved for the royal family.

The church is an important venue for
concerts of classical music. It also has a
Brass Rubbing Centre and a good café.
The churchyard outside is the burial site
of Charles II's mistress Nell Gwynn,
William Hogarth and Joshua Reynolds.

WHITEHALL

Leave Trafalgar Square and head south
down Whitehall, named after Henry
VIII's palace, which burnt down in
1698. Most of the monumental buildings on this street are government
departments, beginning with former
Admiralty buildings on your right and
the Ministry of Defence on your left.

Horse Guards
Soon, on the right, through the arch,
is **Horse Guards ④**, where the
Household Cavalry – the Queen's
bodyguard on state occasions – mount
a picturesque daily ceremony known as
Changing the Guard (www.changing-
the-guard.com; Mon–Sat 11am, Sun
10am; free). Cameras click, horses nod,
commands are shouted, and the troop
returns to its barracks.

Banqueting House
On the opposite side of Whitehall from
Horse Guards is the **Banqueting
House ⑤** (tel: 020-7930 4179; www.
hrp.org.uk; Mon–Sat 10am–5pm;
lunchtime concerts on first Mon of
every month except Aug; charge). It
was built by Inigo Jones for James I as
part of Whitehall Palace in 1619–22

and was probably London's first
building made of Portland stone, and
first in the Classically influenced style
of the 16th-century Italian architect
Andrea Palladio. It must have looked
astonishingly avant-garde among the
Tudor timber-and-brick buildings surrounding it (these burnt down in 1698).

Inside, the Rubens ceiling provides a
robust contrast to the restraint of the
exterior. Commissioned by Charles I to
glorify his father James I, it celebrates
the divine right of the Stuart kings.
However, a bust over the entrance commemorates the fact that Charles was
beheaded just outside in 1649.

Downing Street
On the opposite side of the road, and
further along, is **Downing Street ⑥**,
home to the prime minister of the day
since 1732. Traditionally, the prime
minister lives at no. 10, and the chancellor at no. 11; however, William
Gladstone and family, during his last
period in office in 1881, occupied nos
10, 11 and 12. Since 1989, steel gates
have closed the street to the public for
security reasons.

PARLIAMENT SQUARE

Now continue down Whitehall, passing,
on your right, the **Foreign Office**,
designed by George Gilbert Scott in
Italianate style and completed in 1868,
before coming to Parliament Square.

On your left is the **Palace of Westminster ⑦**, where the two Houses of
Parliament (the House of Lords and
the House of Commons) meet. Visitors

can attend debates, watch judicial hearings and committees, and take guided tours of the building (general information: tel: 020-7219 4272; tours: tel: 0870 906 3773; www.parliament.uk; charge). Tickets may be available on the day from the office next to the Jewel Tower in Old Palace Yard, opposite.

Monarchs from Edward the Confessor (1003–66) to Henry VIII (1491–1547) have had residences at this location, which is still a royal palace. The oldest part surviving today is Westminster Hall, the walls of which date from 1097; once used as a law court, it was the scene of the trial of the Gunpowder Plot conspirators in 1606. Henry VIII also apparently used it for playing tennis.

The rest of the old palace was almost completely burnt down in a fire in 1834 – the crypt of St Stephen's Chapel and the Jewel Tower survived. Rebuilding took just over 30 years, according to the Neo-Gothic plans of Sir Charles Barry and A.W. Pugin.

During World War II, however, a bombing raid destroyed the chamber of the House of Commons, so architect Sir Giles Gilbert Scott was commissioned to design the replacement. Today the vast building contains nearly 1,200 rooms, 100 staircases and more than 2 miles (3km) of corridors.

Westminster Abbey

Across the road from the Houses of Parliament, on the south side of the square, is **Westminster Abbey** ❽ (tel: 020-7222 5152; www.westminster-abbey.org; Main Abbey Church: Mon, Tue, Thur, Fri 9.30am–3.45pm, Wed 9.30am–6pm, Sat 9.30am–1.45pm; Chapter House and Museum: daily 10.30am–4pm; Cloisters: daily 8am–

Above from left: statue of Oliver Cromwell; the lavish House of Lords.

First UN Assembly West of Parliament Square is the dome of Westminster Central Hall. Now used for conferences and Methodist services, in 1946 it hosted the first assembly of the United Nations. South of the Hall is a good lunch option, see ⑪②.

Big Ben

At the northern end of the Palace of Westminster is the Clock Tower, standing 96m (316ft) tall. It was Pugin's last design before his descent into madness and death. It houses five bells, which strike the Westminster Chimes every quarter hour. The largest of these, which strikes the hour, is Big Ben, the third-heaviest bell in England, weighing 13.76 tonnes. The name 'Big Ben' properly refers only to this bell, but is often used to refer to the whole tower. The huge clock (the faces are 23ft/7m in diameter) is famous for its reliability. It is fine-tuned with a small stack of old penny coins on its pendulum: adding or removing a penny changes the clock's speed by two fifths of a second per day. UK residents can arrange to climb Big Ben – apply to your MP or to a Lord. A 20-ft (6-m) replica, known as Little Ben, stands on a traffic island near Victoria Station.

Food and Drink ⑪

② CINNAMON CLUB

30–2 Great Smith Street; tel: 020-7222 2555; Mon–Fri B, L and D, Sat L and D; £££–££££
More like a colonial club than the Old Westminster Library it once was. The haute-cuisine take on Indian cooking is innovative and tasty, and the wines complement the spicy food well.

Above from left:
Westminster Abbey;
member of the Life
Guards; Chelsea
Pensioner in St
James's Park in
spring; ornamental
gate to Green Park
on the Mall.

Tombs of the Great
As well as kings,
Westminster Abbey
became, from early
on, the burial place
of aristocrats and
monks. These
included Geoffrey
Chaucer, who, in the
centuries since, has
gathered around him
kindred spirits (Lord
Tennyson, Thomas
Hardy, etc) to form
Poets' Corner. The
practice was then
extended to others,
including politicians
(Pitt, Gladstone,
Attlee, etc), com-
posers (including
Purcell and Handel)
and scientists (Isaac
Newton, Charles
Darwin, et al.).

6pm; charge). The medieval abbey on this site was completed and consecrated in 1065, only a week before Edward the Confessor's death. He, along with almost all monarchs since, was buried here. King Harold and William the Conqueror were subsequently crowned here on St Edward's Chair – again, as have most monarchs since.

Henry III rebuilt the abbey in the 13th century, and only the Pyx chamber (royal treasury) and undercroft remain of the original. The fan-vaulted Henry VII Chapel was added from 1503 to 1512, and architect Nicholas Hawksmoor built the west towers in 1745.

Among the church's many relics and monuments *(see left)* is St Edward the Confessor's burial vault, rediscovered in 2005 beneath the mosaic pavement, before the High Altar. Also of note is the Chapter House, with its fine 13th-century tiled pavement, and, further on, the Little Cloister and College Garden.

St Margaret's

Next door is the official church of the House of Commons, **St Margaret's** ❾ (tel: 020-7654 4840; Mon–Fri 9.30am–3.45pm, Sat 9.30am–1.45pm, Sun 2–5pm; free). Inside, the fine east window (1526) commemorates the marriage of Henry VIII and Catherine of Aragon, while the west window (1888) is a tribute to Sir Walter Raleigh (1552–1618), executed for treason nearby. He is buried in the chancel.

Cabinet War Rooms

Leaving Parliament Square by Great George Street, you come to the edge of St James's Park. Turn right, and on the corner of King Charles Street are the **Cabinet War Rooms** ❿ (tel: 020-7930 6961; cwr.iwm.org.uk; daily 9.30am–6pm; charge), the underground bunker from where Winston Churchill masterminded his World War II campaign.

Little has changed since it was closed on 16 August 1945; every book, map, chart and pin remains in place, as does the BBC microphone Churchill used for his famous wartime broadcasts. There is even a telephone scrambler system, concealed as a lavatory; this gave the prime minister a hotline to the White House. A museum displays the great man's red velvet romper suit, Bowler hat, champagne and cigars.

ST JAMES'S PARK

Now stroll into **St James's Park** ⓫ (tel: 020-7298 2000; www.royalparks.org. uk; daily 5am–midnight; free). Henry VIII first formed it by draining a swamp; Charles II decked it out in French style with a straight canal; and George IV, with architect John Nash, put a bend in the lake, gave it an island and also a bridge with some of the best views in London. Today, the park is a favourite lunching spot for civil servants from nearby government offices – if you are peckish too, consider stopping at **Inn the Park**, see ⑪③.

THE MALL

Emerging from the park on its northern perimeter, you find yourself on the pink tarmac of The Mall, the processional

route running from Aston Webb's **Admiralty Arch** (1912) to his **Queen Victoria Memorial** (1911) in front of Buckingham Palace. The road was originally laid out by Charles II when he wanted a new pitch for *pallemaille* (Pall Mall, his favourite pitch, had become too crowded). This was a popular game of the time, and involved hitting a ball through a hoop at the end of a long alley.

Carlton House Terrace

Almost opposite where Horse Guards Road joins The Mall, is a grand staircase leading up to Nash's **Carlton House Terrace** ⑫. This complex, completed in 1835, was built on the site of the recently demolished mansion of the Prince Regent (later George IV; *see p.46*), who had decided to move to a revamped Buckingham House (later 'Palace').

The enormous column in between the two sections of terrace is a tribute to 'The Grand Old Duke of York' of the children's nursery rhyme. The duke was in fact commander-in-chief during the French Revolutionary Wars. The memorial was paid for by stopping a day's pay from all ranks of the army.

ICA

Tucked under Carlton House Terrace on the Mall is the **Institute of Contemporary Arts** ⑬ (tel: 020-7930 3647; www.ica.org.uk; daily noon-late; charge), with a gallery, cinema, bar-restaurant (see ⑪④) and bookshop. It was founded in 1948 by art critic Herbert Read, with a remit to challenge traditional notions of art.

St James's Palace

Walking down The Mall towards Buckingham Palace, on your right you pass the garden walls of **Marlborough House**, built by Christopher Wren from 1709 to 1711. It was the home of Queen Mary, grandmother of the present Queen, until her death in 1953. Adjacent, on Marlborough Road, is the Queen's Chapel, designed by Inigo Jones; its interior can be viewed during Sunday services, from Easter to July.

Next on your right is **St James's Palace** ⑭ (closed to the public). This castellated brick building was commissioned by Henry VIII, but only became the principal residence of the monarch in London from 1698, when Whitehall Palace burnt down. This is where Mary I died, Elizabeth I waited for the Spanish Armada to sail up the channel, and Charles I spent his final night before being executed. It is now the administrative centre of the monarchy.

Associated with this palace complex is **Clarence House** (access from The Mall; tel: 020-7766 7303; guided tours only,

Guards Museum

On the southern perimeter of St James's Park is Birdcage Walk, where James I once had his aviary, but where you can now visit the Guards Museum (tel: 020-7414 3428; daily 10am–4pm; charge) in Wellington Barracks. It illustrates the history of the British Army's five Guards regiments with uniforms, paintings and medals, and you can even try on a Guardsman's Bearskin Cap. The museum shop sells toy soldiers.

Food and Drink 🍴

③ INN THE PARK

North-east Section of St James's Park; tel: 020-7451 9999; daily B, L and D; self-service area: £–££; formal restaurant: £££–££££

Kedgeree or a full English for breakfast, grilled halibut for lunch, scones with clotted cream for afternoon tea (when the pelicans are fed outside at 3pm) and lamb chops for dinner. Self-service snacks also available. Interior by Tom Dixon. Service sometimes slow.

④ ICA BAR

12 Carlton House Terrace (entrance on The Mall); tel: 020-7930 0493; daily L and D; ££

The bar attracts a lively, arty crowd. Food, served till late, includes good burgers, enchiladas and salads.

The Royal Mews
Visit the Royal Mews on Buckingham Palace Road (mid-Mar–Oct: Sat–Thur 11am–4pm, Aug and Sept 11am–5pm; charge) to see the Queen's horses, carriages and motor cars used for coronations, state visits, weddings and other events. See the Coronation Coach, built for George III in 1762, visit the stables of the horses (mainly Cleveland Bays and Windsor Greys) and admire the footmen's lavish costumes.

Aug and Sept daily 10am–5.30pm; charge), the residence of Prince Charles and his sons, William and Harry, and formerly (1953–2002), the home of the Queen Mother, whose art collection and family mementoes are still in place.

BUCKINGHAM PALACE

Now, continue to the forecourt of **Buckingham Palace** ⑮ (tel: 020-7766 7300; www.royalcollection.org.uk; State Rooms open Aug and Sept only 9.45am–6pm, last admission 3.45pm; beat the queues by buying tickets in advance online; charge). Originally the country house of the Duke of Buckingham (hence the name), the building was bought in 1761 by George III for his wife, Queen Charlotte. George IV came to the throne in 1820 and had the mansion transformed into a palace by the architect John Nash. By 1829, however, the costs had risen to £500,000, and Nash was replaced by Edward Blore to finish the work.

On completion, the first monarch to move in was Queen Victoria, in 1837. Remarkably, she soon found there were no nurseries and too few bedrooms, so a fourth wing was built. The palace finally came into its present state in

1914, when the weathered façade was redesigned by Sir Aston Webb.

In front of the Palace, Changing the Guard takes place daily as at Horse Guards (www.changing-the-guard.com; May–July: daily at 11.30am; Aug–April: alternate days at 11.30am – see website for details; free). Here, the ceremony is accompanied by music from the Guards' band and takes 40 minutes.

The State Rooms
The Palace has 775 rooms, including 52 royal and guest bedrooms, 188 staff bedrooms and 78 bathrooms. In summer, when the Queen stays at Balmoral Castle in Scotland, the State Rooms (used regularly by the Queen for state banquets, receptions and ceremonies) are open to the public. The sumptuous interiors feature paintings by Rembrandt, Vermeer, Poussin and Canaletto, as well as fine sculpture and furniture.

Queen's Gallery
Further along Buckingham Palace Road from the entrance to the State Rooms is the **Queen's Gallery** (tel: 020-7766 7301; daily 10am–5.30pm; charge). This displays selections from the royal art collection, including numerous royal portraits (notably by Holbein and Van Dyck), paintings by Rembrandt, Rubens and Canaletto, and drawings by Leonardo, Holbein, Raphael, Michelangelo and Poussin.

From here the nearest tube is at Victoria, south-west down Buckingham Palace Road. For the **Vincent Rooms**, see ⑪⑤, head down Buckingham Gate, Artillery Row and Rochester Road.

Food and Drink 🍴
⑤ THE VINCENT ROOMS
Westminster Kingsway College, Vincent Square; tel: 020-7802 8391; Mon–Fri L noon–1.15pm, Tue–Thur D 6–7.15pm; closed July–Sept, 2 weeks in Apr and 2 weeks Dec–Jan; ££–£££
Britain's top catering college (where Jamie Oliver trained) serves the day's lesson to the paying public. Quality ingredients, often superb execution, pleasant surroundings and reasonable prices.

NATIONAL GALLERIES

In a Neoclassical building with a 'pepperpot' dome, looking out over Trafalgar Square, is one of the world's finest art collections, displaying about 2,300 masterpieces dating from the mid-13th century to 1900. Adjacent is a gallery devoted to the national collection of portraits.

This tour takes in two of London's most important art galleries, and looks at their collections in detail. The walk can easily be combined with tour 1 *(see p.24)*, which starts at Trafalgar Square.

THE NATIONAL GALLERY

The **National Gallery** ❶ (tel: 020-7747 2885; daily 10am–6pm, Wed till 9pm; free) was founded in 1824, when a private collection of 38 paintings was acquired by the British Government for the sum of £57,000 and exhibited in the house of the late owner, banker John Julius Angerstein, at 100 Pall Mall. This modest beginning contrasted starkly with grand princely institutions such as the Louvre in Paris or the Prado in Madrid.

The Move to Trafalgar Square

Before long, a more suitable home for the growing collection was sought. The solution came with William Wilkins' long, low construction, opened in 1834 on the then-recently created Trafalgar Square. From the start, however, the building has been criticised as being somewhat inadequate, and additions ever since have done little to confront the shortcomings.

> **DISTANCE** ½ mile (0.25km) not incl. distance covered in galleries
> **TIME** Half a day
> **START** National Gallery
> **END** National Portrait Gallery
> **POINTS TO NOTE**
> At peak times these galleries can be crowded. Good times to visit include Sunday mornings and the last hour or so on evenings when the galleries open late; on hot summer weekends, the galleries can also be quiet. This tour combines easily with walk 1.

The Sainsbury Wing

In 1991 a major extension, the Sainsbury Wing, was built to provide much-needed facilities: new galleries, a lecture theatre, restaurant, shop and space for temporary exhibitions. It was designed by the North American architect Robert Venturi to harmonise with the rest of the building, while offering a humorous comment on its Classical idiom. A previous, more avant-garde proposal had been scrapped after Prince Charles's now-famous denouncement of it as 'a monstrous carbuncle on the face of a much-loved and elegant friend'.

Above: logo and royal crest on the railings outside the National Portrait Gallery.

World War II
At the outbreak of war in 1939, the National Gallery's paintings were hidden in Manod Quarry in North Wales after Prime Minister Winston Churchill's instructions, 'bury them in caves or in cellars, but not a picture shall leave these islands'.

Art Attack

In 1914 a campaigner for women's suffrage took a knife to Velázquez's *Rokeby Venus*, in protest against the arrest of Emmeline Pankhurst. Later, after another suffragette attacked five Bellini paintings, it was decided to close the gallery until the start of World War I, when the Women's Social and Political Union called an end to the protests.

Below: Velázquez's *Rokeby Venus*.

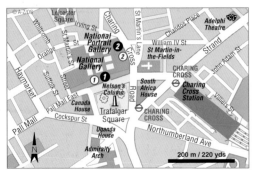

Tour of the Collection

The National Gallery's collection is arranged chronologically, from the 13th century to the end of the 19th, through four wings, starting in the Sainsbury Wing, which contains works from the 13th to 15th centuries. Starting here means resisting the temptation to go into the gallery through its grand main entrance (from where a magnificent staircase offers you a choice of three directions), but it makes sense in terms of the chronology.

Highlights here include medieval and earlier Renaissance works, among them Van Eyck's *The Arnolfini Portrait* (1434), Piero della Francesca's *The Baptism of Christ* (1450s) and the jewel-like *Wilton Diptych* (1395–9) by an unknown artist.

Renaissance Galleries

From the Sainsbury Wing, take the walkway east towards the main building's West Wing and the Renaissance galleries. Here, rooms 2 to 12 harbour masterpieces such as Raphael's *The Madonna of the Pinks* (1506–7), recently purchased for £22 million; Leonardo da Vinci's *The Virgin of the Rocks* (1491–1508); and Holbein's *The Ambassadors* (1533), with its image of a skull – distorted when viewed from the front, but mysteriously corrected when viewed from the side.

North Wing

From either room 9 or 14 (in the West Wing), you can access the North Wing, which houses paintings from 1600 to 1700. Here you will find works by Caravaggio and Rubens, self-portraits by Rembrandt and equestrian portraits by Van Dyck. Always worth seeking out are Vermeer's quiet and enigmatic *A Young Woman standing at a Virginal* (*c.*1670–2) and Velázquez's more exuberant *Rokeby Venus* (1647–51), the Spanish painter's only surviving nude.

East Wing

In the East Wing are paintings advancing the story of art from 1700 right up to the threshold of modernity. From the aristocratic portraits of Gainsborough and the rural backwaters of John Constable's landscapes (including *The Hay Wain* of 1821), you soon find yourself, a few rooms on, confronted by the optical innovations of Seurat's *Bathers at Asnières* (1884), the vibrant colours and violent emo-

tions of Van Gogh's *Sunflowers* (1888) and the hints of Cubism in Cézanne's *Bathers* (*c*.1894–1905).

After all that, you can now recuperate in the Gallery's excellent café immediately below, on Level 0, see ⑪①.

NATIONAL PORTRAIT GALLERY

Tucked behind the National Gallery, just to the north-east, on St Martin's Place, is the **National Portrait Gallery** ❷ (tel: 020-7306 0055; daily 10am–6pm, Thur and Fri till 9pm; free except special exhibitions), which is full of famous British faces.

Background

A British historical portrait gallery was founded in 1856, the initiative of the 5th Earl of Stanhope. With no collection as such, it relied on gifts and bequests, the first of which was the 'Chandos' picture of William Shakespeare (*c*.1610), attributed to John Taylor and arguably the only portrait of Britain's most famous playwright done from life.

From the start, additions to the collection (initially comprising traditional paintings, drawings and sculpture, with photography a later addition) were determined by the status of the sitter and historical importance of the portrait, not by their quality as works of art; these criteria still pertain today. Portraits of living people were not admitted until 1968, when the policy was changed in order to encourage younger artists and a fresh exploration of the genre.

The Collection

The stylish galleries display portraits of important British people past and present. The displays are broadly chronological, starting on the second floor (reached by the vast escalator from the ticket hall) and ending on the ground floor. There are thematic subdivisions within each period: the Tudors and 17th- and 18th-century portraits on the second floor; the Victorians and 20th-century portraits (to 1990) on the first floor; and, on the ground floor, the ever-popular British portraits since 1990 and (usually) excellent temporary exhibitions.

Highlights include self-portraits by Hogarth and Reynolds, Patrick Branwell Brontë's painting of his literary sisters Charlotte, Emily and Anne, and numerous royal portraits. The contemporary galleries have a curiosity value for seeing how today's celebrities are being recorded for posterity.

When you feel sated with art, head up to the third floor for a cocktail or two in the gallery's chic restaurant, see ⑪②.

Above from far left: J.M.W. Turner's *The Fighting Temeraire* (1839), National Gallery; gallery sign; Alfred Tennyson (*c*.1840) by Samuel Laurence, National Portrait Gallery; *Pauline Boty* (1963) by Michael Seymour, shown as part of the 'British Pop and the 60s Art Scene' 2008 special exhibition.

Below: treats at the National Gallery's National Café.

COVENT GARDEN AND SOHO

East of Charing Cross Road is Covent Garden: once London's fruit-and-vegetable market, it is now a shopping mecca. West of Charing Cross is Soho, which hosts many excellent restaurants and pubs, as well as a thriving gay scene, Chinatown, plenty of cinemas and plenty of sex shops.

Hanky Panky

In the 18th century Covent Garden was a hotbed of prostitution. Courtesans and madams rented the upper rooms of the elegant houses around the piazza, and punters even had their own guidebook, Jack Harris's *List of Covent Garden Ladies*, which sold over 250,000 copies.

DISTANCE 2 miles (3km)
TIME A full day
START Covent Garden tube
END Leicester Square
POINTS TO NOTE

Note that many shops in central London are open until late on Thursdays (usually until around 8pm), so it may be a good idea to walk the retail-heavy Covent Garden half of this route at that time.

The first half of this walk takes you through the district of Covent Garden. It acquired its name during the reign of King John (1199–1216) as the kitchen garden of Westminster Abbey (or Convent) and became a major producer of fruit and vegetables in London over the next three centuries.

In 1540, however, Henry VIII dissolved the country's monasteries, appropriated their land, and formed the Church of England, which, with himself at its head, would be more amenable

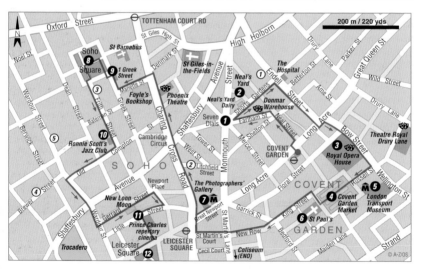

to his frequent changes of wife. Henry granted Covent Garden to Baron Russell, later the first Earl of Bedford.

In the early 17th century, the fourth Earl of Bedford commissioned Inigo Jones to redevelop the area, creating much of the streetplan you see today, as well as the piazza, colonnades and church. Before long a fruit-and-vegetable market here was thriving, and over the next 250 years, it became the most important in the country.

By the 1970s, though, the congestion of central London had become too much and the market moved south of the river. The 1980s brought a revival, and the district was reinvented as a shopping, eating and tourist hub. Today, the area is equally renowned for its shopping, bars and nightclubs, and eccentric street entertainers.

COVENT GARDEN

From **Covent Garden tube station**, turn right on to Long Acre, with its high-street chain stores, and then immediately left on to Neal Street, which is lined with fashion-forward boutiques. Here, you can buy designer streetwear, natural shoes, baskets, kites, China tea, chic toiletries, handbags and jewellery and the latest trainers.

Turn left on to Earlham Street, where, on your right at no. 41, is the **Donmar Warehouse** (booking tel: 0870 060 6624; www.donmarwarehouse. com), one of London's most innovative theatres. Continue along Earlham street to the tiny roundabout known as **Seven Dials ❶**, the junction of seven streets,

then turn right on to Shorts Gardens. At nos 21–3 is an eccentric water-driven clock above the window of a health-food shop. Less healthy, but also excellent, is Neal's Yard Dairy, a cheese shop at no. 17; this marks the entrance (on the left) to **Neal's Yard ❷**, which is otherwise healthfood central – a triangle of shops selling all manner of health foods as well as offering restorative holistic treatments.

Continue up Shorts Gardens, across Neal Street again, and turn right on to Endell Street. Just nearby you can pick up some old-fashioned British grub at the acclaimed **Rock & Sole Plaice**, see ⑪①. Further down Endell Street, on your left at no. 24, is **The Hospital**, a heavily designed art gallery and members' club created by the pop group Eurythmics' Dave Stewart and Microsoft's Paul Allen.

Royal Opera House

Crossing over Long Acre again, you hit Bow Street, home of the 'Bow Street Runners', the forerunners of the police, and the former Magistrates' Court, where Oscar Wilde was convicted in 1895 for committing 'indecent acts'.

Haunted Theatre
From Bow Street, turn left on to Russell Street, and you will find the Theatre Royal Drury Lane on your right. Vulnerable to fire, like the Opera House nearby, this is the fourth theatre to have been built on this site since 1663. With many Georgian features, the ghost-haunted theatre has seen a procession of great names: David Garrick, Sheridan, Kean, Sarah Siddons and Nell Gwynn, the local girl who first sold oranges on opening nights, then became an actress, and finally won King Charles II's heart.

Food and Drink 🍴
① ROCK & SOLE PLAICE

47 Endell Street, Covent Garden; tel: 020-7836 3785; daily 11.30am–11.30pm, Sun till 10pm; £
London's oldest fish and chip shop (est. 1871). The master-fryer offers up the catch of the day (sometimes even mullet or dover sole). Sit inside or out, and if you like, bring your own wine.

Above from left:
Transport Museum; sandal at Paul Smith; the market; bookshop, Charing Cross Road.

Talent Spotting
In *My Fair Lady* Professor Higgins discovers Eliza Doolittle selling flowers at Covent Garden market while he waits for a cab home from the opera. It was also here that the 15-year-old Naomi Campbell was spotted by a model scout as she strolled around the market.

Below: market interior and toy shop.

Located directly opposite is the **Royal Opera House ❸** (Bow Street; tel: 020-7304 4000; www.royalopera house.org; free admission to the Floral Hall, charge for backstage tours). Now home to the Royal Opera and Ballet companies, the theatre was founded in 1728 with the profits from *The Beggar's Opera* by John Gay. Since then it has experienced highs and lows, from staging premieres of Handel's operas to being twice burnt down. It is currently riding high after renovation in the 1990s, and, aside from performances, you can now have lunch here, drink in the bar, view exhibitions and take in views of London's skyline from the magnificent Floral Hall.

Covent Garden Market

Walking around the side of the Opera House, down Russell Street, you come to **Covent Garden Market ❹**. Originally the convent garden of Westminster Abbey, the site came into the possession of the Earls of Bedford, who commissioned Inigo Jones to design a new residential estate in the 1630s. Houses in the terraces facing the square were set above arcades as in the elegant rue de Rivoli in Paris, and the fruit-and-vegetable market was established here not long afterwards. It continued until 1974, when it was moved to Nine Elms on the South Bank near Vauxhall.

The Covered Market

The market building was redesigned by Charles Fowler in 1830. In the North Hall is the Apple Market, which hosts antiques stalls on Mondays, and arts and crafts from Tuesday to Sunday. Surrounding it are speciality shops such as Pollock's, which sells old-fashioned toy theatres among other amusements. The Punch & Judy pub nearby is a reminder that Punch's Puppet Show was first performed here in 1662, as witnessed by Samuel Pepys, the contemporary diarist.

London Transport Museum

In the south-east corner of the square is the **London Transport Museum ❺** (tel: 020-7565 7298; www.ltmuseum.co. uk; Sat–Thur 10am–6pm, Fri 11am–9pm; charge). Newly reopened, the expanded museum deals with all aspects of London travel, from vehicles and

uniforms to signs and posters. Look out in particular for the A Class steam locomotive which hauled passenger trains on the first London Underground line from 1866 until electrification in 1905.

St Paul's Church

On the western side of the square is **St Paul's ❻** (tel: 020-7836 5221; www.actorschurch.org; Mon–Fri 8.30am–5.30pm, Sun 9am–1pm; free). In 1631, the Earl of Bedford commissioned Inigo Jones to build the church, reportedly on a tight budget, prompting the architect's remark, 'You shall have the handsomest barn in England!' Now known as the 'Actors' Church', for its association with the many theatres in the parish, it contains memorials to Charlie Chaplin, Noel Coward, Vivien Leigh and Gracie Fields.

CHARING CROSS ROAD

Walk down King Street, to the right of the church as you face it, and, at the crossroads, continue on to the pedestrianised New Row. When you reach St Martin's Lane (where the ENO is located, *see right*), cross over and walk through St Martin's Court. Then turn right on to Charing Cross Road.

This major road, linking Trafalgar Square with Tottenham Court Road, is traditionally the preserve of London's booksellers. Many have now been forced out by the high rents, but a few remain, including several antiquarian dealers. Try Cecil Court, the next pedestrianised alley to the south from St Martin's Court, for Hogarth prints,

Victorian folding maps of London, vintage theatre posters, modern first editions and sheet music.

The Photographers' Gallery

As you head north up Charing Cross Road, on your right (just past The Porcupine pub) is Great Newport Street. Here, in a house once owned by Joshua Reynolds, is **The Photographers' Gallery ❼** (tel: 020-7831 1772; www.photonet.org.uk; Mon–Sat, 11am–6pm, Thurs till 8pm, Sun noon–6pm; free). On the ground floor is a café with large trestle tables and delicious home-made cakes, while upstairs you can buy limited edition prints by Lartigue, Lee Miller or George Rodger. A space for temporary photographic exhibitions is situated a couple of doors down the street.

Continuing north on Charing Cross Road, next on your right is Litchfield Street, where **Le Beaujolais** is located, see ⑪②. Further up, past Cambridge Circus and on the left, is **Foyle's** bookshop (once the world's largest). Then just afterwards is Manette Street, named after Charles Dickens' Dr Manette in *A Tale of Two Cities* and a fitting introduction to Soho, where many French émigrés settled after the Revolution.

Food and Drink 🍴

② LE BEAUJOLAIS

25 Litchfield Street; tel: 020-7836 2955; Sun–Fri L and D, Sat D only; ££
Noisy, cramped and chaotic, yet friendly, fun and unpretentious, this wine bar serves French bistro fare (and vegetarian options) to the accompaniment of blues and jazz.

ENO
At the southern end of St Martin's Lane is the Coliseum, home to English National Opera (ENO; St Martin's Lane; tel: 0870 145 0200; www.eno.org). While performances at the Royal Opera House (Covent Garden) are sung in the vernacular, here they are usually in English. Tickets are cheaper than those at Covent Garden, and can often be bought on the night.

Denmark Street
On the other side of Charing Cross Road from Manette Street is Britain's Tin Pan Alley, where songwriters and music publishers worked in the 1950s and '60s. The Beatles and Jimi Hendrix made recordings here, Elton John wrote *Your Song*, and, the Sex Pistols lived at no. 6. The street is now lined with music stores.

Above from left:
in one of Chinatown's many Chinese restaurants; dim sum; Covent Garden and Soho are good for lingerie boutiques; Old Compton Street, the focus of London's gay community.

Tally Ho!
The name Soho is believed to derive from the hunting cry 'so-hoe', a legacy of its former role as a hunting ground.

SOHO

Bounded by Regent Street, Charing Cross Road, Oxford Street and Leicester Square, Soho embodies the myths of both 1960s 'swinging London' and its more recent, 1990s, ironic version, 'cool Britannia'. Although the maze of narrow streets may not quite live up to the promise of either, there is a definite buzz to the district, helped by the presence of part of London's gay and lesbian scene, as well as a cluster of youthful media companies.

Before the 17th century, however, this was all open fields, and used as a hunting ground. The first streets to be developed were Old Compton, Gerrard, Frith and Greek streets, laid out in the 1670s by bricklayer Richard Frith.

Today these streets are lined with bars, restaurants and clubs, and remain busy almost around the clock. Despite this being one of London's major nightlife centres, what you see is still a considerably cleaned-up version of the old louche Soho, although there are still remants of a red-light district, tucked away on the quieter streets.

Soho Square and Greek Street

Back at Manette Street, where you entered Soho, turn right into Greek Street and walk up to **Soho Square ❽**. A statue of Charles II shares the square with a ventilation shaft heavily disguised as a half-timbered cottage. Most of the 18th-century houses around the square have been surrendered to television, PR and advertising companies, but **no. 1 Greek Street ❾** (tel: 020-7437 1894; Wed 2.30–4pm, Thur 11am–12.30pm) has been preserved by the House of Charity. Even if you do not want to go in – or if the house is closed – its cantilevered 'crinoline' staircase and rococo plasterwork can be glimpsed through the windows.

Frith Street

Now head south from Soho Square via Frith Street. At no. 6, the critic and essayist, William Hazlitt (1778–1830), uttered his last words, 'Well, I've had a happy life,' which should please those staying at the hotel now using the building. Opposite is **Arbutus**, see ⑪③, and, beyond, on the corner of Bateman Street, the Dog and Duck pub, with its exuberant Victorian decoration.

Further down, at no. 21, is the house where the paying public came in 1765 to see the nine-year-old Mozart play,

---

Food and Drink 🍴

③ ARBUTUS
63–4 Frith Street; tel: 020-7734 4545; daily L and D, pre-theatre dinners from 5pm; ££
Award-winning restaurant that offers remarkable value, especially at lunchtimes. All the wines, no matter how expensive, are available by the glass or carafe. The modern European food is tasty and imaginatively cooked. Booking essential.

④ RANDALL & AUBIN
16 Brewer Street; tel: 020-7287 4447; daily L and D; ££
Named after the old delicatessen that inhabited this spot for 90 years, Randall & Aubin has inherited a feeling of shopping bustle. Piles of lobster, crabs and oysters greet you as you enter.

⑤ BUSABA EATHAI
106–10 Wardour Street; tel: 020-7255 8686; daily L and D; £–££
Stylishly designed Thai restaurant, with a convivial atmosphere, in part due to the communal tables. Serves fresh Thai cooking at reasonable prices, with good vegetarian options.

thereby replenishing his father's coffers. Opposite, at no. 18, you can test your own musical abilities at **Karaoke Box Dai Chan** (tel: 020-7494 3878). A few doors along at no. 22 is **Bar Italia**, which is open till fashionably late, though otherwise impervious to trends. This building is where John Logie Baird gave the first public demonstration of television in 1926.

On the other side of the road, at no. 47, is **Ronnie Scott's Jazz Club ❿** (tel: 020-7439 0747; www.ronniescotts.co. uk), where Count Basie played, Ella Fitzgerald sang, and Jimi Hendrix gave his last public appearance.

Around Old Compton Street
At the end of Frith Street, turn right on to Old Compton Street, the focus of Soho's gay scene. If you need a pit-stop at this point, continue to the end of Old Compton Street and carry on straight over at the crossroads for Brewer Street and **Randall & Aubin**, see ⑪④, a lively seafood restaurant sandwiched between sex shops and Italian delicatessens.

Chinatown
Back on Wardour Street, a little to the north, is the popular, dependable **Busaba Eathai**, see ⑪⑤, while, if you follow the street south, across Shaftesbury Avenue, there is the **Wong Kei**, at nos 41–3, an almost comic multistorey Chinese restaurant, with famously brusque staff and cheap, yet not so cheerful, food.

Turn left soon afterwards on to **Gerrard Street**, which is Chinatown's main thoroughfare. At no. 9 is the **New Loon Moon supermarket**, housed in an 18th-century purpose-built brothel. Opposite, at no. 43, is the **New Loon Fung supermarket**, once home to the poet John Dryden (1631–1700).

Leicester Square
At the end of Gerrard Street, turn right at Newport Place, then right again into Lisle Street. Turn left at the good, cheap **Prince Charles repertory cinema ⓫** (tel: 0870 811 2559; www. princecharlescinema.com) on Leicester Place to reach **Leicester Square ⓬**. Here, by the city's largest cinemas – a frequent venue for film premieres – the route ends.

French Connection
In the 17th century the Huguenots started arriving in Soho as religious refugees. Today, there is still a French Protestant Church here, at nos 8–9 Soho Square. Meanwhile, the Roman Catholic French church is on Leicester Place. Built in the 1950s (its predecessor was bombed in 1940), it has murals by Jean Cocteau and mosaics by Boris Anrep.

Below: retro scooters lined up in Soho.

PICCADILLY AND MAYFAIR

The heart of the West End presents grand thoroughfares, glorious churches and fine art galleries. But beware: you will need your credit card handy for this route, since it takes in some of London's most exclusive shopping streets.

Dracula's House
In Bram Stoker's 1897 novel, *Dracula*, the vampire count buys the house at no. 347 Piccadilly. Unfortunately, the house numbers do not go up that high, and the address is merely fictitious.

DISTANCE 2¼ miles (3.5km)
TIME Half to a full day
START Piccadilly Circus
END Oxford Street
POINTS TO NOTE
If you are merely interested in taking in the sights, this route could comfortably be completed in half a day. If, on the other hand, you are a keen shopper, the timescale could extend indefinitely, as you shop between sights.

Not for nothing is Mayfair the most expensive square on the London Monopoly board. This is the area for five-star hotels, art dealers, Bentley showrooms, offices of hedge funds and haute-couture stores. Running east-west on its southern edge is Piccadilly (smart St James's is to the south), while Oxford Street, the capital's high street, runs along the north boundary. On the western border is Park Lane (the second most expensive square on the Monopoly board).

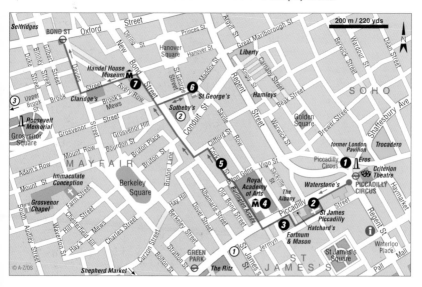

Regent Street

Forming the eastern boundary of Mayfair, curving northwards from Piccadilly Circus, is **Regent Street**, Britain's first purpose-built shopping street, designed by John Nash and completed in 1825. It was built to link the future George IV's residence at Carlton House in St James's to Regent's Park, and is still part of the Crown Estate today. Although the present route will take you down Piccadilly itself, worthwhile destinations on Regent Street for another time include the toyshop Hamley's, Art Nouveau Liberty & Co., and the BBC's Broadcasting House, beyond Oxford Street.

PICCADILLY CIRCUS

Coming out of Piccadilly tube station, you enter the melée of **Piccadilly Circus ❶**. Above are the famous neon billboards; the first electric advertisements appeared here in 1910.

The porticoed building on the northeastern side of the circus, the **London Pavilion**, was built as a music hall in 1859; sadly today it is a rather uninspiring shopping centre. On the south side is the more appealing **Criterion Theatre**, designed by Thomas Verity and opened in 1874; after refurbishment, it is once again putting on plays.

Eros

In the centre of the circus is a fountain topped with a statue known as **Eros**. It was erected in 1892–3 to commemorate Lord Shaftesbury, a Victorian politician who campaigned for better conditions in factories and coal mines, for mental health provision and child welfare. Despite its name, the aluminium statue is actually of Eros's twin, Anteros. The sculptor Alfred Gilbert chose Anteros as the embodiment of selfless love, using a 16-year-old Italian boy as his model.

PICCADILLY

Leaving Piccadilly Circus, walk along Piccadilly. The street's name is thought to have come from the 'piccadill', the stiff collars you see in portraits of Elizabeth I or Sir Walter Raleigh, and made by a 17th-century local tailor, Robert Baker. On the south side of the street is the flagship branch of Waterstone's, supposedly the largest bookshop in Europe. The Art Deco building was formerly occupied by Simpsons department store, the model for the television sitcom, *Are You Being Served?*

St James Piccadilly

A little further down is the church of **St James Piccadilly ❷** (tel: 020-7734 4511; daily; free), designed by Christopher Wren and consecrated in 1684. Seek out inside the carved work of Grinling Gibbons: the fine limewood reredos and the marble font (in which the poet William Blake was baptised).

Shopping

Directly behind the church is **Jermyn Street**, lined with London's finest shirtmakers and gentlemen's outfitters. Take a look there before returning to Piccadilly, where the next stretch of the road offers equally interesting shop-

Above from far left: elegant Berkeley Square; bespoke tailoring; Eros; teddies at Hamley's.

The Albany
Next to the Royal Academy is this fine mansion built from 1770–4 to designs by Sir William Chambers. In 1802 it was converted into chambers for gentlemen, bachelors and those with no connections with trade. Past residents include Lord Palmerston, Gladstone, Byron, Macaulay, the fictional Raffles, Aldous Huxley, Graham Greene, Isaiah Berlin, Terence Stamp, Edward Heath and the diarist Alan Clark.

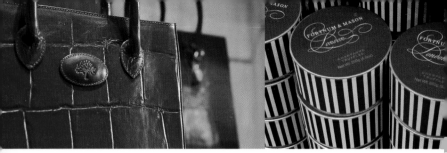

Above from left:
leather at Mulberry; truffles at Fortnum and Mason; posh arcade; Shepherd Market.

Burlington Arcade
The calm in this upmarket shopping arcade was shattered in 1964 when a Jaguar Mark X sped down it, scattering pedestrians. Six masked men leapt out, smashed the windows of the Goldsmiths and Silversmiths Association shop, and stole jewellery valued at £35,000. They were never caught.

ping opportunities. At no. 187 is the bookshop **Hatchard's**, which has operated on this site since 1801. The young Noël Coward was caught shoplifting here in 1917, packing books into a stolen suitcase. A few doors down is **Fortnum and Mason ❸**, grocers to the royal family. Even if you do not want to buy anything here, it is worth popping in for its beautifully preserved Edwardian interior. Further along again is another gorgeous interior, this time a restaurant, the **Wolseley**, see ⑪①, for refreshment at any time of day.

Royal Academy of Arts

On the opposite side of Piccadilly is Burlington House, home of the **Royal Academy of Arts ❹** (tel: 020-7300 8000; daily 10am–6pm, Fri till 10pm; charge), founded in 1768. A statue of its first president, the painter Joshua Reynolds can be seen in the front courtyard. The Academy's main function today is the staging of large exhibitions of great art from the past. There is also an annual summer exhibition of new art, to which anyone can submit pictures for inclusion; the best are selected and are available for purchase.

From the Royal Academy, walk through Burlington Arcade, just adjacent on the right-hand side. Watch out for the 'Beadles', guards who patrol this haven of luxury boutiques in their traditional uniforms of top hats and tailcoats.

MAYFAIR

Emerging from the arcade you will find yourself on Burlington Gardens, in Mayfair. Off to the right is Savile Row, where bespoke tailors create the finest men's suits in the world, while to the left are the fashion emporia of exclusive Bond Street. Immediately in front of you, however, is Cork Street.

Commercial Art Galleries

Cork Street ❺ is one of the streets in London (others include Dover Street, Dering Street and Bond Street, all nearby), where the top art dealers cluster. Major galleries on this street include Bernard Jacobson at no. 6 and Waddington's at no. 11. Among the most successful artists represented here are Frank Stella, Robert Indiana, Peter Blake and Howard Hodgkin.

Food and Drink 🍴

① THE WOLSELEY
160 Piccadilly; tel: 020-7499 6996; daily B, L and D; £££
This place was built as a car showroom in 1921, converted into a posh branch of Barclay's Bank in 1927, then a restaurant in 2003. The interior is exceptional, and the breakfasts (including omelette Arnold Bennett – made with haddock, mustard and cheese), all-day menu for snacks (even steak tartare) and afternoon tea (nice cakes) are delicious. Lunch and dinner are also good, though booking is advisable.

② SOTHEBY'S CAFÉ
34–5 New Bond Street; tel: 020-7293 5077; Mon–Fri 9.30am–5pm; ££
For a reasonable-value breakfast, lunch and afternoon tea in an expensive neighbourhood, bear in mind the surprisingly unstuffy café on the ground floor of this venerable auction house.

③ LE GAVROCHE
43 Upper Brook Street, Mayfair; tel: 020-7408 0881; Mon–Fri L and D, Sat D only; ££££
Chef Michel Roux Jr offers haute-cuisine in the grand style, and the three-course set lunch at £48, including half a bottle of wine per person, coffee and water, is a bargain. Undoubtedly one of London's best restaurants.

Bond Street

At the end of Cork Street turn left on to **Bond Street**, where you will find exclusive couturiers and designer boutiques (Chanel, Gucci, Prada, etc), jewellers (Asprey, Boucheron, Bulgari), as well as art and antiques galleries. The southern half of the street is the more upmarket. At nos 34–35 is the headquarters of **Sotheby's**, the famous auctioneers founded in 1744. Members of the public are free to enter and watch an auction or view the items for sale. There is also an excellent café, see ⑪②.

Walking north up Bond Street, a short detour off to the right on Maddox Street brings you to **St George's Church ❻** (tel: 020-7629 0874; Mon–Fri 8am–4pm, Sun 8am–noon; free), built 1721–4 by architect John James. George Frederick Handel was a regular worshipper here and, much later, it was the venue for the weddings of George Eliot as well as Teddy Roosevelt.

Brook Street

Back on Bond Street, further up and this time off to the left is Brook Street. At no. 25, among more luxury goods shops, is the **Handel House Museum ❼** (tel: 020-7495 1685; Tue–Sat 10am–6pm, till 8pm on Thur, Sun noon–6pm; charge), where the composer of *The Messiah* lived from 1723 until his death in 1759. Next door, and much later (1968–9), lived a very different sort of musician – Jimi Hendrix – commemorated by a blue plaque.

Further up Brook Street is **Claridge's**, one of the city's smartest hotels. Chef Gordon Ramsay runs the hotel restaurant, and it is much easier to get a reservation here than for his flagship Chelsea restaurant. Perhaps even better, though, is **Le Gavroche**, see ⑪③, further up still, on Upper Brook Street.

Oxford Street

Turning north up Davies Street (opposite Claridge's) you emerge on to **Oxford Street**. This is London's high street, where, as well as souvenir shops, there are big department stores, notably Selfridges, John Lewis and House of Fraser. When you have had enough of shopping, escape via one of the tube stations on the street: from west to east, Marble Arch, Bond Street, Oxford Circus or Tottenham Court Road.

Shepherd Market

Off Piccadilly, down White Horse Street, is this pretty square with a clutch of good pubs, and places for alfresco dining (especially L'Artiste Musclé, at no. 1 Shepherd Market). This used to be the scene of the annual May Fair (after which the district is named), held here from 1686 until 1764, when it was banned in this location because of riotous behaviour.

Below: bright lights at The Ritz.

MARYLEBONE

In contrast to hectic, overtly commercial Oxford Street directly south, elegant Marylebone exudes a calm villagey air. This walk takes you along its main artery, with art, waxworks and Victorian sleuthing along the way.

Wigmore Hall
On the north side of Wigmore Street is the Art Nouveau Wigmore Hall (booking tel: 020-7935 2141; www. wigmore-hall.org.uk), erected in 1901 as a venue for recitals of classical chamber music. The concerts at 11.30am every Sunday are popular with music aficionados, and breakfast in the café downstairs is an equally big draw.

> **DISTANCE** 1¼ miles (2km)
> **TIME** Half a day
> **START** Bond Street tube
> **END** Baker Street
> **POINTS TO NOTE**
> Visit Madame Tussauds after 5pm to cut the price and queuing time. Do the walk on Sunday if you want to visit Moxon Street's farmers' market.

The need to relieve congestion in Oxford Street in the early 18th century inspired the building of a new road from Paddington to Islington through the parish of St Mary-by-the-bourne. The

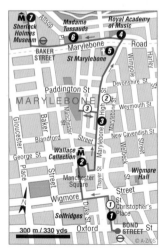

wealthy Portman family funded the development of the adjacent district: Marylebone (pronounced 'mar-le-bun'), which retains many of its smart Georgian buildings and genteel ambience.

ST CHRISTOPHER'S PLACE

From **Bond Street** tube, cross to the other side of Oxford Street and walk north up the narrow **St Christopher's Place ❶**, a relaxed pedestrian enclave, full of boutiques and cafés, including **Carluccio's**, see ⑪①.

North of St Christopher's Place is Wigmore Street, where medical specialists spill over from nearby Harley and Wimpole streets, the domains of private physicians since the 1840s.

WALLACE COLLECTION

Turn left on Wigmore Street, then second right on to Duke Street, which leads to Manchester Square. On the opposite side of the square is Hertford House and the **Wallace Collection ❷** (tel: 020-7563 9500; www.wallace collection.org; daily 10am–5pm; free).

Bequeathed to the British nation by the widow of Richard Wallace, the illegitimate son of the fourth Marquess of Hertford, the collection comprises paintings, furniture, porcelain and a

surprisingly large amount of armour. Highlights include works by Boucher, Fragonard, Watteau, Franz Hals (notably his *Laughing Cavalier),* Rembrandt and Rubens. The gallery has a restaurant in the glazed-over courtyard.

THE HIGH STREET

Turn left as you leave the gallery and take Hinde Street east off the square. Turn left at the crossroads and walk up Thayer Street, which becomes **Marylebone High Street ❸**. This strip has the feel of a well-heeled urban village, with its chic boutiques, non-mainstream bookstores (the Oxfam Bookshop at no. 91 and Daunt Books at nos 83–4), gourmet delicatessens and hip cafés, including **Quiet Revolution**, see ⑪②.

Just over half way up, on the left, is Moxon Street and the **Fromagerie**, see ⑪③; on Sundays a farmers' market (10am–2pm) is held here. Back on the high street, at no. 55, is the Conran Shop, set in a former stables; opened in 1999, the shop sparked the area's regeneration and rise to fashionability.

MARYLEBONE ROAD

At the top of Marylebone High Street is the east-west artery, **Marylebone Road**. Straight ahead is the **Royal Academy of Music ❹** (tel: 020-7873 7300; www.ram.ac.uk; museum: Mon–Fri 11.30am–5.30pm, Sat, Sun noon–4pm), which hosts concerts (mostly free) and is home to a museum of historic instruments and archive material.

Opposite is **St Marylebone ❺**, the fourth church on this site. The second was depicted by William Hogarth in his 18th-century *Rake's Progress.*

Madame Tussauds

Walk west at this point for **Madame Tussauds ❻** (tel: 020-7935 6861; www. madame-tussauds.co.uk; daily 9am–6pm; charge). Expect to queue before being able to mingle with and even touch the wax and silicone doppelgängers, some more convincing than others. The stress is on contemporary celebrities and bizarre special effects.

BAKER STREET

Now continue further west for Baker Street. At no. 239 is the **Sherlock Holmes Museum ❼** (tel: 020-7935 8866; www.sherlock-holmes.co.uk; daily 9.30am–6.30pm; charge), which recreates the home of Sir Arthur Conan Doyle's fictional super-sleuth.

Madame Tussaud Marie Grosholtz prepared death masks of victims of the French Revolution of 1789. She left her husband of seven years, François Tussaud, in 1802 to spend 33 years touring Britain with a growing collection of wax figures. The current museum dates to 1884.

Food and Drink

① CARLUCCIO'S
St Christopher's Place; tel: 020-7935 5927; Mon–Fri 8am–11pm, Sat 9am–11pm, Sun 9am–10.30pm; ££
Antonio Carluccio's flagship 'caffe'-cum-deli makes the most of the location with attractive outdoor seating. Light, fresh Italian fare.

② QUIET REVOLUTION
28–9 Marylebone High Street; tel: 020-7487 5683; Mon–Sat 9am–6pm; Sun 11am–5pm; £–££
At the back of the Aveda shop is this laid-back organic café serving healthy food. Trestle tables add to the friendly atmosphere.

③ LA FROMAGERIE
2–4 Moxon Street; tel: 020-7935 0341; Mon 10.30am–7.30pm, Tue–Fri 8am–7.30pm, Sat 9am–7pm, Sun 10am–6pm; ££–£££
The café at the back of this upmarket cheese shop does inventive, seasonal salads, wholesome soups and fine cheese plates.

REGENT'S PARK

The extravagance of the Prince Regent led to the building of Regent's Park, worth visiting for its rose gardens, boating lake and zoo, as well as Regent Street, which linked the park to his home, Carlton House, on The Mall.

DISTANCE 2½ miles (4km)
TIME Half to a full day
START Regent's Park tube
END London Zoo
POINTS TO NOTE

For an alternative way to reach the park, take the canal boat from Camden Lock or Little Venice along Regent's Canal. The London Waterbus runs regular services in summer (tel: 020-7482 2660; www.londonwaterbus.com); reduced service in winter.

Diorama

At 18 Park Square East is the entrance to what was once the Diorama, a three-storey glass-roofed octagonal auditorium (it can be viewed from Peto Place round the corner). Designed by Augustus Pugin senior, it consisted of an auditorium for 200 people which could be rotated 73 degrees to view either of two stages. *Trompe-l'oeil* scenes were painted on calico cloths 72ft (22m) high and included Canterbury Cathedral and a Swiss Alpine valley. Special effects were created with music and lighting. Sadly, it was not a great success with the public and closed in 1851.

Regent's Park (tel: 020-7486 7905; www.royalparks.org.uk; daily 5am–dusk; free) was originally part of Henry VIII's hunting chase around London. It began to take on its current form in 1811, when the Prince Regent (1762–1830; the future George IV) took control and hired John Nash as architect. Of Nash's original scheme, not everything was realised: his summer palace was never built, and only eight (two survive) of 56 villas for the Prince's friends were erected; however, his terraces, churches, barracks and river were all put in place.

The park became home to the Zoological, Royal Toxophilite (archery) and Royal Botanic societies, and opened to the public in 1835. A century later Queen Mary's Gardens were added.

NASH'S TERRACES

Emerging from **Regent's Park tube station** at the centre point of Nash's Park Crescent, fortify yourself with breakfast or lunch at the RIBA Café, see ⑪① (Portland Place is due south and on the left). Walk back up again and cross the busy road to Park Square East, where formerly you would have entered the **Diorama ❶** *(see left)*. At the square's north-east corner is St Andrew's Place, dominated by the Royal College of Physicians, the arch-modern masterpiece – completed in 1964 – of architect Denys Lasdun.

Walk up the Outer Circle past **Cambridge Gate ❷**, built in 1880 on the site of the Colosseum – a domed building designed by Decimus Burton in 1827 and which housed a panorama of London painted on 40,000 sq ft (3,716 sq m) of canvas; it did not attract enough visitors and was demolished in 1875.

Next along is patrician Chester Terrace: walk through the middle of this via **Chester Gate ❸**. To the right of the archway is a small villa and, mounted on the wall, the bust of a man with 'round head, snub nose, and little eyes' – Nash's description of himself. Emerging from the archway at the end of the terrace, turn left and cross over the Outer Circle to enter the park.

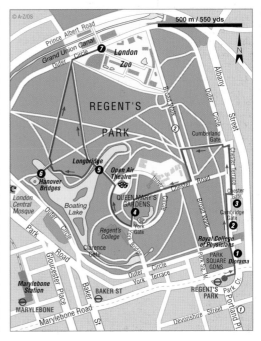

QUEEN MARY'S GARDENS

Follow the path straight on into the park until you reach the **Broad Walk**, lined with benches. Turn right for the **Honest Sausage**, see ⑪②. Turn left, then right on Chester Road, for the **Inner Circle** and **Queen Mary's Gardens ❹**, with their 400 varieties of rose and water gardens, and, on the far side, a café and the open-air theatre (tel: 0870 060 1811; www.openairtheatre.org; summer only).

THE LAKE

Rejoining the Inner Circle at York Gate, walk clockwise round to the path for **Longbridge ❺**, which leads over the lake. This is where Trevor Howard and Celia Johnson went boating in David Lean's classic British romantic movie, *Brief Encounter* (1945). If you think you could do better than Howard, follow the path along the far side of the lake to the **Hanover Bridges ❻**, where boats can be hired (summer: 9am–8pm, winter: 10am–4pm; charge).

LONDON ZOO

To visit **London Zoo ❼** (tel: 020-7722 3333; www.zsl.org; Mar–Oct: daily 10am–5.30pm, Oct–Feb: daily 10am–4pm; charge), founded in 1828, take a path north from either Longbridge or the Hanover Bridges. At the Outer Circle turn right for the zoo's main entrance. The zoo is particularly famous for its gorillas, of which there are currently three: Bobby, Zaire and Effie. They have recently been given a nice new enclosure. Note that the best time to visit is feeding time in the afternoon, especially for the penguins and chimpanzees.

Food and Drink

① RIBA CAFÉ
66 Portland Place; tel: 020-7631 0467; daily B, L and D; ££
Stylish 1930s setting in the headquarters of the Royal Institute of British Architects. Fresh, light meals.

② THE HONEST SAUSAGE
The Broadwalk, Regent's Park; no tel; www.honestsausage.com; daily 8am–7pm, winter till 4pm; £
This lodge serves high-quality free-range pork sausages from a family-run Gloucestershire butcher in a range of settings (eg on mash, in roll, next to egg, etc); 'guest' sausages sometimes feature. Sausages apart, try the bacon butties, salads, soups and sandwiches (classic fillings such as egg and cress, and cheddar).

BLOOMSBURY

This is the brainy part of town. For Indiana Jones types there's the British Museum, for literary Bloomsberries there's the houses of Charles Dickens or Virginia Woolf, and for boffins there's the University of London.

Above: bookish cat in literary Bloomsbury.

Tube Station Mosaic
Look out for the brightly coloured mosaics by pop artist Eduardo Paolozzi in Tottenham Court Road station.

DISTANCE 2 miles (3km)
TIME A full day
START British Museum
END Russell Square
POINTS TO NOTE

The nearest tube station to the British Museum is Tottenham Court Road. To reach the starting point from here, leave the tube station by the exit for the Dominion Theatre, walk north up Tottenham Court Road, then turn right into Great Russell Street. Just after the crossroads with Bloomsbury Street, the British Museum is on your left. The museum is vast and you will probably need at least half a day to explore it.

Food and Drink

① BRITISH MUSEUM CAFÉ
Great Court, British Museum; Sun–Wed B, L and T 9am–5.30pm, Thur–Sat B, L and D, till 9pm; £
Snacks, sandwiches and drinks in the unique setting of the Great Court, with its magnificent roof by Norman Foster. There is also a smart restaurant upstairs for lunch and afternoon tea daily, plus dinner on Thur and Fri (tel: 020-7323 8990; £££).

② TRUCKLES
Pied Bull Yard, Off Bury Place; tel: 020-7404 5338; Mon–Fri L and D 11am–10pm; ££–£££
Traditional Ale and Port House in a courtyard next to the London Review of Books Bookshop. Simple and modern upstairs; candle-lit tables and sawdust-covered floors downstairs; seating outside in summer. Dishes include dressed crab, lamb shank and treacle tart; note also the 30-minute set lunch (£10).

Bloomsbury is bounded to the north by Euston, St Pancras and King's Cross railway termini, but this is no typical station hinterland. It is the hotbed of London's intellectual activity: it was home to the Bloomsbury literati of the early 20th century, and still has a distinctly cultural and academic atmosphere, as home to both the British Museum and the University of London.

BRITISH MUSEUM

The **British Museum ①** (tel: 020-7323 8299; www.the britishmuseum.ac.uk; daily 10am–5.30pm, selected galleries open until 8.30pm Thur and Fri; free) is one of the oldest museums in the world, founded by an Act of Parliament in 1753 and opened in 1759. It has accumulated a collection of 6.5 million objects. Devote just 60 seconds to each and you would be there for more than 12 years. Although only 50,000 objects are on display, this is not a place to rush through in an hour. It is also one of the most visited attractions in London and the best time to go is soon after opening. As there are so many things to see, we cover the highlights below, so that you can prioritise, according to interest.

Note that options for refreshments in or near the museum include the

museum cafe, see 🍴①, in the Great Court, redesigned by architect Norman Foster. Alternatively, head for **Truckles**, see 🍴②, by leaving the museum, then turning left, crossing over and taking a right turn on to Bury Place; Truckles is in a courtyard just on your left.

Egyptian Mummies: Rooms 62–3

By far the biggest crowd-puller in the museum are the Egyptian sarcophagi. Thanks to enthusiastic plundering by 19th-century explorers, the collection (located on the upper floor) is the richest outside Egypt.

Rosetta Stone: Room 4

Another big attraction is the 2nd-century BC granite tablet known as the Rosetta Stone, which provided the key for deciphering Egyptian hieroglyphics. In the same room is the colossal sandstone head of pharaoh Rameses II, said to be the inspiration for *Ozymandias*, Shelley's poem on the transience of power.

Elgin Marbles: Room 18

Among the museum's more controversial holdings are the Elgin Marbles, which represent the high point of ancient Greek art. Carved in the 5th century BC, they depict the battle of the Lapiths and Centaurs, a festival procession for the Goddess Athena, as well as various Greek gods.

The marbles were taken from the Parthenon temple on the Acropolis in Athens by Lord Elgin in the early 19th century. His action, ironically, saved them for posterity, since the acropolis

temples were employed for storing munitions during the Greek War of Independence (1821–33) and much of what remained was reduced to ruin. Understandably, the Greeks want the sculptures returned.

Benin Bronzes: Room 25

In the basement are around five dozen of the 900 brass plaques found in Benin City, Nigeria, in 1897. The Benin Bronzes were probably cast in the 16th century to clad the wooden pillars of the palace; they depict court life and ritual in extraordinary detail.

Anglo-Saxon Ship Burial: Room 41

The Sutton Hoo Ship Burial was the richest treasure ever dug from British soil. The early 7th-century longboat was probably the burial chamber of Raedwald, an East Anglian king. The acidic sand had destroyed all organic material well before the excavation in 1939, but

Above from far left: the British Museum's Great Court; ancient Egyptian sarcophagus at the British Museum.

The Portland Vase
This Roman glass masterpiece (room 70) was made in c.20BC. In 1845 however, it was smashed by a drunken vandal. Crudely glued back together soon afterwards, it has recently been taken apart again and expertly reassembled. It now looks as good as new.

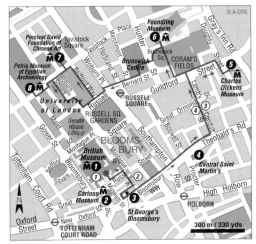

a rich hoard of weapons, armour, coins, bowls and jewellery survived.

Other Highlights

In room 42 are the Lewis Chessmen, found on the Isle of Lewis in Scotland's Outer Hebrides and probably made in Norway. These 12th-century chess pieces are elaborately carved from walrus ivory and whales' teeth, The helmeted figures and faces set in curious scowls are almost comical.

Room 50 exhibits the preserved corpse of Lindow Man, the victim of a sacrifice, who was found in a peat bog in Cheshire in 1984. Scientists were able to determine his blood group, what he looked like and what he had eaten.

HISTORIC STREETS

When finished at the museum, walk down Bury Place and turn right at Little Russell Street. Follow this road across Museum Street to stop in at the **Cartoon Museum ②** on your right at no. 35 (tel: 020-7580 8155; www. cartoonmuseum.org; Tue–Sat 10.30am–5.30pm, Sun noon–5.30pm; charge). Alternatively, browse in the bookshops and galleries on Museum Street before continuing the route by turning left on to Bloomsbury Way at the bottom of the street.

Almost immediately on your left is the church of **St George's Bloomsbury ③** (tel: 020-7405 3044; Tue–Fri 1– 2pm, Sat 11.30am–5pm, Sun 2–5 pm; free), the sixth and final (completed 1731) London church designed by Nicholas Hawksmoor, the leading

architect of the English Baroque. The steeple is in the form of a stepped pyramid surmounted by Britain's only statue of George I.

Continuing along Bloomsbury Way, cross over Southampton Row on to Theobald's Road. On your right is **Central Saint Martin's ④** (tel: 020-7514 7015), one of London's top art colleges, with its own museum and collection of work by staff, students and alumni. Further on – the fifth turning on your left – is Lamb's Conduit Street, full of shops, attractive pubs, cafés and restaurants, including **Cigala** and **Vat's Winebar**, see ⑪③ and ⑪④. Continue to the end of the street, then turn right at Guildford Place and right again on to Doughty Street.

DICKENS MUSEUM

At 48 Doughty Street is the **Charles Dickens Museum ⑤** (tel: 020-7405 2127; www.dickensmuseum.com; Mon–Sat 10am–5pm, Sun 11am–5pm; charge). The author lived here from 1837–9 while writing *Nicholas Nickleby* and *Oliver Twist*. It is the only one of his London homes still standing, and exhibits all manner of memorabilia: his letters, manuscripts, desk, locks of his hair and even his lemon squeezer.

FOUNDLING MUSEUM

Retrace your steps to Guildford Place, where, on your right, is **Coram's Fields**, a children's park (adults admitted only with a child). Facing on to the park on the west side at 40 Brunswick Square

Faber and Faber
T.S. Eliot worked as poetry editor at this famous publisher on Russell Square.

Bloomsbury Group
In the early 20th century, a group of friends, nicknamed the Bloomsberries and including E.M. Forster, Lytton Strachey, J.M. Keynes, Clive and Vanessa Bell, Duncan Grant and Virginia and Leonard Woolf would meet at each other's houses at nos 37, 46, 50 and 51 Gordon Square to discuss literature and art. Other notable Bloomsbury residents have included Thomas Carlyle at 38 Ampton Street, Edgar Allan Poe at 83 Southampton Row, Anthony Trollope at 6 Store Street and W.B. Yeats at 5 Upper Woburn Place.

is the **Foundling Museum** ⑥ (tel: 020-7841 3600; www.foundlingmuseum.org.uk; Tue–Sat 10am–6pm, Sun noon–6pm; charge). Formerly Thomas Coram's Foundling Hospital, it cared for 27,000 abandoned children between 1739 and 1953, when it closed.

As well as telling the hospital's story – with poignant mementos left by mothers for their babies – the museum has important collections relating to two of its first governors, the artist William Hogarth and the composer George Frederick Handel. Hogarth encouraged artists of the day to donate works and, in doing so, created Britain's first public art gallery. The collection includes works by Hogarth, Reynolds and Gainsborough, displayed in the original interiors.

Handel donated proceeds from annual performances of *The Messiah* and bequeathed the manuscripts to the hospital. The museum has since acquired a huge collection relating to Handel, including manuscripts, books and music, libretti and paintings.

UNIVERSITY OF LONDON

Leaving the Foundling Museum, head for the other side of the square and the Futurist-inspired Brunswick Centre, designed by Patrick Hodgkinson in 1973 and recently given a much-needed facelift. Walk up the steps by the Renoir arts cinema and turn left through the complex past the cafés and restaurants to emerge on to Bernard Street. Walk past the tube station and on to Russell Square. Turn right off the

square on Bedford Way and you are in university territory.

At the end of the street, turn left, and across the road is the first of two university museums, the **Percival David Foundation of Chinese Art** ⑦ (tel: 020-7387 3909; Mon–Fri 10am–12.30pm and 1.30–5pm; free). Inside are rare ceramics and paintings.

Continue west from Gordon Square on to Byng Place to find Malet Place, an inconspicuous lane on your right, leading into University College and the **Petrie Museum of Egyptian Archaeology** ⑧ (tel: 020-7679 2884; www.petrie.ucl.ac.uk; Tue–Fri 1–5pm, Sat 10am–1pm; free). Look out inside for the world's oldest dress (2800BC).

Finally, return to Russell Square, and the tube, by turning right off Gordon Square, cutting through Woburn Square and turning left.

Food and Drink 🍴

③ CIGALA
54 Lamb's Conduit Street; tel: 020-7405 1717; L and D daily; £££
Buzzing neighbourhood Spanish restaurant offering tapas or à la carte dishes under the aegis of owner-chef Jake Hodges (ex-Moro in Clerkenwell). Excellent sherries, wines and liqueurs. Good-value set lunch menus.

④ VAT'S WINEBAR
51 Lamb's Conduit Street; tel: 020-7242 8963; Mon–Fri L and D; £££
Well-established and perennially popular winebar. In a comfortable wooden-panelled interior, the friendly staff serve comforting food to accompany the serious wine list. Expect hearty portions of pork belly, pheasant casserole and lamb shank.

University Library
In World War II, the Senate House Library on Russell Square was used as the Ministry of Information. Hitler then earmarked it for his post-invasion HQ. It was also the model for the Ministry of Truth in George Orwell's *1984*.

Wellcome Collection
North of the university, opposite Euston Station, is the excellent Wellcome Collection (183 Euston Road, www.wellcomecollection.org; Tue–Sat with late opening Thur; free), a museum/art space devoted to medicine and its relationships with art and society. It mixes items from Henry Wellcome's (1853–1936) eclectic collection of objects, interactive exhibits, paintings and more. Other draws include a café and bookshop.

Bowling Alley
Go ten-pin bowling in style in the basement of the Tavistock Hotel on Bedford Way (tel: 020-7691 2610; www.bloomsburybowling.com). This is a great option for children on a wet day, but note that they are not admitted after 4pm. In the evenings and at weekends it is advisable to book.

HOLBORN AND
THE INNS OF COURT

This area is the domain of journalists and lawyers so vividly described in the novels of Charles Dickens. The atmosphere is well preserved in the winding backstreets, rickety old pubs, quaint shops and historic churches.

Early Printing

Printing and publishing grew up around Fleet Street in the 15th century. The new industry located here because it was an enclave of the clergy: as the clergy had a near monopoly on literacy, they were the printers' best customers.

DISTANCE 2 miles (3km)

TIME Half to a full day

START St Bride's, Fleet Street

END Somerset House

POINTS TO NOTE

The walk may take a whole day if you visit all the museums on the route.

The nearest station to the starting point above is Blackfriars Station (rail and tube). Leave by exit no. 8 and walk north to reach Fleet Street.

The nearest tube station to Somerset House is Temple on the Embankment.

This tour starts at the western end of Fleet Street, a strip synonymous with print journalism, although the industry has long since moved out. To continue where many a hack left off, set yourself up for the tour with a stop at the **Blackfriar**, see ①, one of the many historic watering holes in this part of London, opposite Blackfriars Station. When sated, walk north to Ludgate Circus, then turn left on to Fleet Street to follow the bank of the old Fleet River, which is now buried in a sewer.

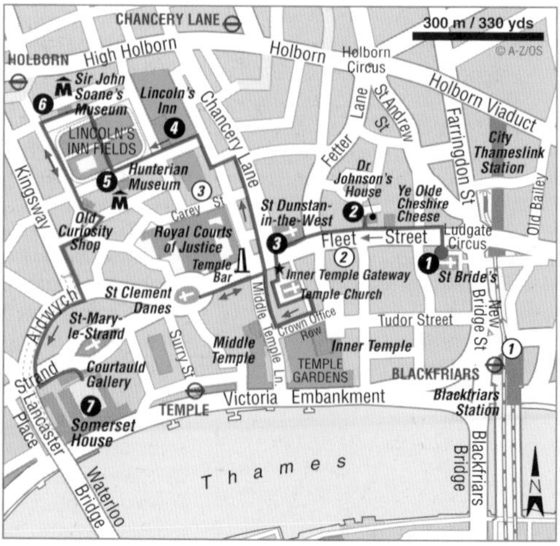

FLEET STREET

On the left, down Bride Lane, rises the steeple of **St Bride's ①** (tel: 020-7427 0133; Mon–Fri 8am–6pm, Sat 11am–3pm, Sun 10am–1pm and 5–7.30pm; free). This church, the inspiration for the first tiered wedding cake, was built by architect Sir Christopher Wren after the Great Fire of London destroyed its medieval predecessor in 1666. Unfortunately, the church was gutted again during the Blitz in 1940, though it has been carefully restored. A museum in the crypt displays Roman mosaics, Saxon church walls as well as a product of England's first printing press, William Caxton's *Ovid*.

Offices of National Newspapers

On the other side of Fleet Street are the former offices of Britain's national newspapers, which relocated in the 1980s to cheaper, high-tech sites, notably Wapping in the Docklands. At no. 121 is an Art Deco building of black glass and chromium (nicknamed Black Lubyanka), which was once the nerve-centre of the Express Newspapers. A few doors down, the pillared palace at no. 135 used to house the *Telegraph*.

Dr Johnson's House

On the same side of the road, look out for **Ye Olde Cheshire Cheese** pub (rebuilt 1667), once frequented by Samuel Johnson and his cronies, including Oliver Goldsmith, who lived at no 6. From here it is just a short, well-signposted, walk to **Dr Johnson's House ❷** on Gough Square (tel: 020-7353 3745; www.drjohnsonshouse.org; Mon– Sat 11am–5.30pm, till 5pm in winter; charge). Johnson lived here from 1748 to 1759, compiling his dictionary in the garret with six poor copyists. Outside the house is a statue of Johnson's pet cat, Hodge: 'a very fine cat indeed'.

Returning to Fleet Street, cross the road to **El Vino**, see ⑪②.

Church of St Dunstan-in-the-West

On the other side of Fleet Street, just beyond Fetter Lane, is **St Dunstan-in-the-West ❸** (tel: 020-7405 1929; Mon–Fri 11am–2pm; free). It is famous for its 17th-century clock (its two giants strike the hours and quarters), and its association with poet-priest John Donne, who was rector here (1624–31).

Over the porch at the side is a statue of Queen Elizabeth I, the only one known to have been carved during her lifetime.

THE INNS OF COURT

Further along, on the left at no. 17, is the **Inner Temple Gateway**, leading to the quadrangles, chambers and gardens of one of the four Inns of Court. Enter the lane beneath and continue to **Temple Church**, part of which was built in the 1180s for the Knights Templar. Head left across Church Court to King's Bench Walk (where Tony Blair once practised as a barrister) and turn right. Soon, turn right again on to Crown Office Row, and continue past the gardens (Mon–Fri 12.30–3pm; free) to emerge on Middle Temple Lane.

Turn right, passing on your left the buildings of another of the Inns of Court, **Middle Temple**, and you come out at the point where Fleet Street ends

Food and Drink 🍴

① **BLACKFRIAR PUB**

174 Queen Victoria Street, Blackfriars; tel: 020-7236 5474; daily L and D; ££
The interior of this Victorian pub was remodelled in 1902 by Arts and Crafts exponent, Henry Poole. Every inch is covered in marble, mosaic or low-relief sculpture. Wonderful. Decent real ales, reasonable pub food (until 9pm).

② **EL VINO**

47 Fleet Street; tel: 020-7353 6786; Mon–Fri B, L and D; ££–£££
Well-established Fleet Street wine bar with convivial atmosphere and hearty food (of the steak and kidney pie school). Good wines. Very fair prices.

Above from far left: classic watering hole, El Vino; Samuel Johnson; St Bride's ready for court.

Sweeney Todd

Next door to St Dunstan's are the old offices of the Dundee Courier, built on the site of Sweeney Todd's barber shop. In the 1780s, Todd is reputed to have killed over 100 of his clients, and then sold the bodies to Lovett's Pie Shop (in Bell Yard further along) where they were cooked up into meat pies.

Gateway Tavern

On the first floor of the Inner Temple Gateway is Prince Henry's Room (open Mon–Fri 11am–2pm), with the initials of James I's son on the elaborate plaster ceiling. The building, which dates from 1611, was originally a tavern called The Prince's Arms.

Above from left: looking out of the historic Seven Stars pub towards the Royal Courts of Justice; bird's-eye view of the City by night.

Cabbies' Shelter
Turn right at the southern end of Middle Temple Lane and on Temple Place above Embankment is one of the few remaining cabmen's shelters. Once common across London, thanks to the Cabmen's Shelter Fund, set up in 1874, they gave cabbies alternatives to pubs. The green shed was not allowed to take up more space than a horse and cab.

The Silver Vaults
Now home to dealers in fine silver, the London Silver Vaults (tel: 020-7242 3844) at the top of Chancery Lane were opened in 1876 to provide strong rooms for the wealthy to protect their valuables.

and the Strand begins. This, the boundary of the City of London, is marked by **Temple Bar**, a stone monument topped with a dragon. Further west (in the middle of the road) is the church of **St Clement Danes**, built in 1682 by Sir Christopher Wren. It was damaged in the Blitz but then restored as the church of the Royal Air Force.

Chancery Lane

On the far side of the road are the **Royal Courts of Justice**, where England's most important civil law cases are heard. To its right is Chancery Lane. As you walk up, on your left is Carey Street where you can find wigmakers' shops, the Silver Mousetrap jewellers (est. 1690) and the **Seven Stars** pub, see ⑪③, the 'Magpie and Stump' of Dickens's *Pickwick Papers*.

Lincoln's Inn Fields

Further up Chancery Lane, enter **Lincoln's Inn** ❹ through the arch on the left marked 'New Square'. Its more aptly named Old Hall was built during the reign of Henry VII (1485–1509). Walk straight through to the east gate and **Lincoln's Inn Fields**, London's largest

> ## Food and Drink 🍴
> ### ③ THE SEVEN STARS
> 53a Carey Street; tel: 020-7242 8521; daily L and D; ££
> Built in 1602, this pub survived the Great Fire, and, thanks to proprietor Roxy Beaujolais, remains unspoilt to this day. Just by the back door of the law courts, it is popular with lawyers. Good beer and food (oysters, herrings, meatloaf, game stew).

square. On the south side is the Royal College of Surgeons, which houses the **Hunterian Museum** ❺ (tel: 020-7869 6560; www.rcseng.ac.uk; Tue–Sat 10am–5pm; free) with its collection of fine art, as well as anatomical specimens.

Sir John Soane's Museum

On the north side of the square at no. 13 is the eccentric **Sir John Soane's Museum** ❻ (tel: 020-7405 2107; www.soane.org; Tue–Sat 10am–5pm and first Tue of month 6–9pm; free). Soane (1753–1826), best known as the architect of the Bank of England, designed this, his own house. Its rooms are just as he left them: packed with antiquities and paintings, including Hogarth's *Rake's Progress* and *The Election*.

Leave the square by the south-west corner, on Portsmouth Street. **The Old Curiosity Shop** from Dickens's novel is on the left (now selling shoes). Navigate the lanes south to reach Aldwych, which leads back to the Strand.

SOMERSET HOUSE

On the south side is **Somerset House** ❼, a Palladian mansion built by Sir William Chambers from 1776–96, now home to the **Courtauld Gallery** (tel: 020-7845 4600; www.somersethouse.org.uk; daily 10am–6pm; charge, though Mon free), displaying outstanding paintings, from Michelangelo to Monet. Also at Somerset House is the **Gilbert Collection** of silver. In summer, the fountains in the courtyard make way for open-air cinema, while in winter there is an ice rink.

THE CITY

Despite its rich history, the City is no museum. Hi-tech office towers crowd the dome of St Paul's Cathedral, and the Beefeaters at the Tower of London are vastly outnumbered by 300,000 business suits on their daily commute.

The nearest tube to the starting point is Tower Hill. From the tube exit turn right towards the Tower of London. As you walk down the steps of the subway, a section of the old Roman city wall is on your left. On the other side of the road, turn right; the main entrance to the Tower is on the river side.

DISTANCE 2¼ miles (3.5km)
TIME A full day
START Tower of London
END Barbican
POINTS TO NOTE
Walk this route on a weekday, as the City is dormant at weekends.

TOWER OF LONDON

It was in 1078 that William the Conqueror ordered the building of the **Tower of London ❶** (tel: 0844 482 7777; www.hrp.org.uk; Mar–Oct: Tue–Sat 9am–5.30pm, Sun and Mon 10am–5.30pm; last guided tour 3.30pm; Nov–Feb: closes at 4.30pm, last guided tour 2.30pm; charge). Since then, the most haunted building in England has housed a zoo (from the reign of King John, 1199–1216), a palace (under Henry III, 1216–72) and a VIP prison (inmates included Elizabeth I, Guy Fawkes, Walter Raleigh and, more recently, Rudolf Hess).

To see the Tower, you might join one of the hour-long tours led by a Yeoman Warder (a Beefeater). Visit the **White Tower**, the only intact Norman keep left in England, and the armoury, which contains an execution axe and chopping block (two of Henry VIII's wives were beheaded here). See also the **Crown Jewels**, stored here since 1303. As well as crowns, orbs and sceptres, there is a 2-m (6½-ft) wide punchbowl. Outside, watch out for the Royal Ravens: legend has it that if they ever leave, the Tower will crumble. This came close to happening in World War II, when all but one died from shock during bombing raids.

ALONG THE RIVER

If you are now in need of a rest, cross over Tower Bridge Approach on the eastern side of the Tower of London to **St Katharine's Dock ❷**, where you can enjoy a drink at one of the cafés overlooking the marina. Here, Telford's fine warehouses, once piled with ivory tusks, are the backdrop for Thames barges, restored clippers and an 18th-century warship, *The Grand Turk*.

Now, returning to the main entrance of the Tower, walk up Lower Thames

Tower Bridge
Next to the Tower of London is Tower Bridge (tel: 020-7403 3761; www.tower bridge.org.uk; Apr–Sept 10am–6.30pm, Oct–Mar 9:30am–6pm; charge). Completed in 1894, its iconic 1,000-ton bascules are still raised some 1,000 times a year, though now using electricity and oil rather than steam. The high-level walkways – in their early days popular with prostitutes and pickpockets – offer wonderful views to the paying public. In 1952 a London bus had to leap from one bascule to the other, when the bridge began to rise with the bus still on it.

Above from left:
City workers on their
lunch break; St Paul's,
seen from the South
Bank; Sir Christopher
Wren; old and new
architecture in the City.

London Bridge
St Magnus the Martyr
marks the entrance to
the original London
Bridge, a model of
which stands in the
vestibule. Old London
Bridge, lined with 200
shops, was replaced in
1831 by a simpler
granite structure by
John Rennie a little
upstream. However,
the weight caused the
foundations to sink,
and the bridge was
sold in 1968 to an
American entre-
preneur, who rebuilt
it in Arizona. The
replacement is
practical but bland.

Mansion House
Built 1739–52 by
architect George
Dance the Elder, it is
the official residence of
the Lord Mayor of the
City of London. Behind
it is Wren's church of
St Stephen Walbrook,
with its cleverly
constructed dome.

Street, passing **Custom House** (1817) on your left, followed by **Old Billingsgate Market**, which for centuries had supplied London with fish. Further along, again on the left, is Christopher Wren's church of **St Magnus the Martyr ❸**, completed in 1676 (see margin, left).

THE MONUMENT

Just before the bridge, turn right up Fish Street Hill to **The Monument ❹** (tel: 020-7626 2717; daily 9.30am–5pm; charge), a memorial to the Great Fire of 1666, which started in a bakery on Pudding Lane, just nearby. Built by Christopher Wren and Robert Hooke in 1671–7, this 61-m (202-ft) Doric column was designed to double as a scientific instrument, with a central shaft for use as a zenith telescope (a

---

Food and Drink 🍴

① SWEETINGS
39 Queen Victoria Street; tel: 020-7248 3062; Mon–Fri L only; ££–£££
This City institution (operating from this site since 1889) specialises in fish. A classic lunch might involve a pint of Guinness, potted shrimps (with brown bread and butter), smoked haddock (simply cooked with a poached egg on top) and spotted dick for pudding.

② SIMPSON'S TAVERN
Ball Court, 38 Cornhill; tel: 020-7626 9985; Mon–Fri L only; ££–£££
Down an alley off Cornhill, this time-warped tavern has served up hearty pies and stews and puddings (with custard) to Old-School-tie-wearing City gents since 1759.

---

hinged lid in the flaming urn at the top covers the opening). Around this shaft wind 311 steps leading up to a cage (added after several suicides) from where you can admire the view.

BANK OF ENGLAND

At the top of Fish Hill Street turn left, and, after the major junction, bear right up King William Street into the financial heart of the City. On the way, you pass Wren's church of **St Clement Eastcheap** on your right (of the nursery rhyme, 'Oranges and Lemons', renown), then Nicholas Hawksmoor's **St Mary Woolnoth**, also on the right. At the end of the street, as you approach the Bank of England, on your left is **Mansion House** (see left) and, leading off to the west, Queen Victoria Street where **Sweetings**, see 🍴①, is located. Meanwhile, on the right is the **Royal Exchange** (see right), and Cornhill, leading east to **Simpson's Tavern**, see 🍴②.

On the far side of the junction is Britain's central bank, the **Bank of England ❺** (tel: 020-7601 5545; www. bankofengland.co.uk; Mon–Fri 10am–5pm; free). Designed by architect Sir John Soane in 1788, the building has more space below ground than is contained in the 42 storeys of the NatWest Tower (see margin, p.58). Around the corner on Bartholomew Lane is a museum displaying banknotes, gold bars (you can even pick one up), minting machines and examples of firearms once issued to bank branches for defence.

THE GUILDHALL

At the top of Bartholomew Lane, turn left on to Lothbury and continue until, on your right, you come to the City of London's town hall, the **Guildhall ❻** (tel: 020-7606 3030; www.cityoflondon. gov.uk; phone for opening times; free). Built from 1411 on the site of a Roman amphitheatre (the outline of the arena is marked in black on the courtyard in front), this is the only secular stone building to have survived the Great Fire of 1666. Inside is a large medieval hall with stained glass and extensive crypts.

To the rear is the **Guildhall Library** (tel: 020-7332 1868; Mon–Sat 9.30am–5pm; free), founded in the 1420s with a bequest from Richard Whittington, three times City mayor, and later the inspiration for the pantomime character, Dick. Today, it is a reference library specialising in London history. It also houses the museum of the City clockmakers' guild, displaying over 600 fine timepieces (tel: 020-7332 1868; free).

On the right of the square is the **Guildhall Art Gallery** (tel: 020-7332 3700; Mon–Sat 10am–5pm, Sun noon–4pm; charge). The collection possesses Victorian masterpieces by artists such as Millais, Leighton and Landseer, numerous views of the City, and Britain's largest painting, *The Siege of Gibraltar* by John Singleton Copley.

ST PAUL'S CATHEDRAL

Now walk down King Street, opposite the Guildhall, and turn on to Cheapside. Coming up on your left is the first of three Wren churches, that of **St Mary-le-Bow**. Tradition has it that to be a true cockney (East London's old working class), you have to be born within earshot of the sound of the church's bells. Further along, on your right is the church of **St Vedast**. Then finally, on your left, down New Change, is **St Paul's Cathedral ❼** (tel: 020-7246 8357; www.stpauls.co.uk; Mon–Sat 8.30am–4pm; charge).

CITY OF LONDON

College of Arms
South of St Paul's, at the end of Godliman Street, on your left, is the College of Arms (tel: 020-7248 2762; tours by arrangement 6.30pm Mon–Fri; charge), which oversees the coats of arms of the nobility.

Royal Exchange
Opposite Mansion House is the Royal Exchange, founded in 1565 by Sir Thomas Gresham as a centre of commerce. During the 17th century, stockbrokers were not allowed in because of their rude manners, and had to operate from other establishments such as Jonathan's Coffee House on Exchange Alley, to the south, which became the first London Stock Exchange. Today, the Royal Exchange is occupied by various luxury goods shops.

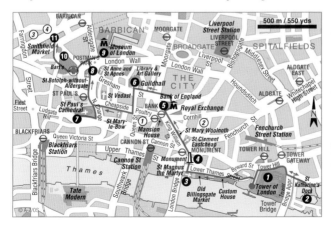

Above from left:
St Paul's, viewed from Ludgate Hill; historic clock by the Royal Exchange; Richard Rogers' Lloyd's Building; Smithfield Market.

City Towers
The tallest building in the City is Tower 42 (formerly known as the NatWest Tower) at 25 Old Broad Street. Designed by Richard Seifert, and built 1971–9, it is 183m (600ft) tall. Second is the Gherkin at 30 St Mary Axe, built by Foster Partners in 2001–4 and 180m (591 ft) tall. Third is CityPoint on Ropemaker Street to the north, at 127m (417ft), built in 1967 and refurbished in 2000.

The cathedral you see today (the fifth on this site) was completed in 1708, on Wren's 76th birthday, after its predecessor was gutted in the Great Fire of 1666. In the later stages of its building, Wren is said to have been hauled up to the rafters in a basket to inspect progress. Inspired by St Peter's Basilica in Rome, the building is centred under a dome rising 108m (354ft) from the floor.

The dome holds three circular galleries. First, up 259 steps is the Whispering Gallery running around the inside of the dome: whisper against its wall at any point, and your voice is audible to a listener with their ear held to the wall at any other point around the gallery. Oddly, speak at a normal volume, and the sound does not transmit in the same way. The ceiling is decorated with monochrome paintings by Sir James Thornhill of scenes from the life of St Paul. The other two galleries are both outside: the Stone Gallery is 378 steps from ground level, and the Golden Gallery, 530 steps up.

If heights are not your forte, visit the cathedral's crypt instead. Christopher Wren was the first to be interred here, in 1723 at the age of 90. Among the famous names that followed were the Duke of Wellington and Lord Nelson, the latter after having been brought back from the Battle of Trafalgar preserved in a barrel of French brandy.

POSTMAN'S PARK

Return now to New Change, head north, and after the crossroads continue on to St Martin's Le Grand, which then becomes Aldersgate Street. On your right is Wren's unusual brick church of **St Anne and St Agnes**, based on the plan of a Greek cross.

Opposite, by the church of **St Botolph-without-Aldersgate** (built by George Dance the Elder in 1725) is the **Postman's Park ❽**, the brainchild of painter and philanthropist George Frederick Watts (1817–1904). It was originally a popular lunchtime spot for workers from the former General Post Office, nearby. It is now noted for its wall covered in Doulton plaques commemorating fatal acts of bravery by the ordinary people of the Victorian era. One memorial reads, 'Thomas Simpson, died of exhaustion after saving many lives from the breaking ice at Highgate Ponds. Jan 25 1885.'

MUSEUM OF LONDON

Further up Aldersgate Street, past the busy roundabout, is the **Museum of London ❾** (tel: 0870 444 3851; www. museumoflondon.org.uk; Mon– Sat 10am–5.50pm, Sun noon–5.50pm; free). This museum takes you from London's earliest beginnings right up to the late 20th century. Highlights include Roman leather 'bikinis', Viking battleaxes, a hoard of Tudor jewellery, dress and costume from royal gowns to Norman Hartnell flapper dresses, paintings from Canaletto to Henry Moore, and the Lord Mayor's gilded coach. There is also a large audio-visual exhibit on the Great Fire, as well as a walk-through Victorian street scene.

BART'S HOSPITAL

From the museum, cross to the other side of the roundabout and walk up Montague Street. Turn right on to Little Britain to enter the complex of **Bart's** ❿. When you emerge on West Smithfield, turn left for the Henry VIII Gate and the historic part of the hospital. Founded in 1123, Bart's is the oldest surviving hospital in England – though all that remains of its medieval fabric is on your left as you enter: the 15th-century chapel of St Bartholomew-the-Less. Walk through the first courtyard for the main square's North Wing, built by James Gibbs in the 1730s. It contains the Baroque **Great Hall** and the **Museum** (tel: 020-7601 8152; Tue–Fri 10am–4pm; free), which offers a history of the hospital as well as access to two spectacular murals (1736–7) by William Hogarth, who used real patients as some of his models.

SMITHFIELD MARKET

On the other side of West Smithfield from the hospital is **Smithfield Market** ⓫, where livestock and meat have been traded since the 10th century. At various times, the site has also been used for jousting, public executions (notably William Wallace's in 1305), the selling of wives and for Bartholomew Fair, which, from 1133 to 1855, drew crowds to its cloth market and pleasure fair. Today, the place is occupied by Sir Horace Jones's market buildings, built from 1866 above railway lines linking farmers and

butchers across the country. The pubs around the market open famously early. In recent years, people tipping out of the area's nightclubs have mingled with market workers over fried breakfasts and pints at 7am. If you are looking to be fed and watered, consider **Comptoir Gascon** or **Vinoteca**, see ⑪③ and ⑪④, on the far side of the market.

St Bartholomew-the-Great
As you come out of Little Britain on to West Smithfield, note this former monastic church (tel: 020-7606 5171; charge), with the finest Norman interior in London.

Food and Drink

③ COMPTOIR GASCON
61–3 Charterhouse Street; tel: 020-7608 0851; Tue–Sat L and D; ££–£££
Comptoir Gascon is an informal, tapas/bistro-style version of the mothership, Club Gascon, on West Smithfield. Cuisine from Southwest France is ably cooked up at both.

④ VINOTECA
7 St John Street; tel: 020-7253 8786; Mon–Sat L and D; ££–£££
Tasty modern European food, together with wines by the glass from a 200-strong list (also retailed from the shop). Recommended.

The Barbican

To the north-east of the Museum of London is the Barbican, a complex comprising 2,000 flats (in London's tallest residential towers) as well as a theatre, concert hall, cinema, art gallery, library, school, YMCA, fire station and even an ornamental lake. It was built by architects Chamberlin, Powell and Bon between 1965 and 1976 on a 35-acre (14-ha) site that had been bombed in World War II. Despite numerous design problems – wind moans through the walkways, it is easy to get lost, the concrete was the wrong type and requires constant maintenance – it is still Britain's finest example of concrete Brutalist architecture; it is unrivalled for its scale, cohesion and attention to detail (from the specially designed carpets to the fitted kitchens).

THE SOUTH BANK

A riverside walk along the southern bank of the Thames, taking in some of the city's most important cultural institutions, as well as Shakespeare's London and the increasingly fashionable area around Borough Market.

Imperial War Museum

An optional detour from this route is the huge Imperial War Museum (Lambeth Road; tel: 020-7416 5320; daily 10am–6pm; free except some special exhibitions), housed in a former hospital for the insane – an inspired choice for a museum that chronicles the horrors of modern war.

DISTANCE 2 miles (3.5km)
TIME Half to a full day
START County Hall
END London Bridge
GETTING AROUND
Allow about half a day for this walk, including one break for refreshments and an hour in one of the museums mentioned. Do the walk on Friday or Saturday if you want to see Borough Market in full swing. This walk is a good choice if you want to avoid London's traffic, as most of the riverside stretch is pedestrianised.

If you arrive by underground, the nearest station to this walk's starting point is Waterloo. From here, leave by the overhead walkway signposted 'Southbank Centre'. At the foot of the steps, you cannot miss the huge London Eye wheel in front of you. Walk towards it.

COUNTY HALL

Start at **County Hall ❶**, which will be on your left as you reach the Eye. Designed in 1908 by architect Ralph Knott and once the seat of the Greater London Council (until it was controversially disbanded by Margaret That-

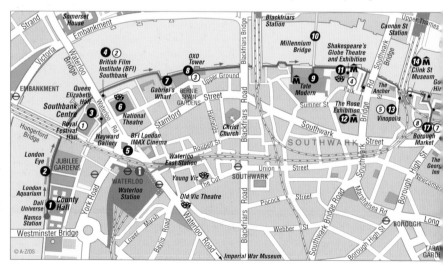

cher's government in 1986), this huge Edwardian Renaissance building is now privately owned and contains two hotels, an aquarium, an art gallery, games arcade and several restaurants.

Namco Station and Dalí Universe

The first attraction you encounter as you walk eastwards along the river is **Namco Station** (tel: 020-7967 1067; 10am–midnight; www.namcostation. co. uk), home to bumper cars, video games and a bowling alley.

Next up is the **Dalí Universe** (tel: 0870-744 7485; daily 10am–5.30pm, later in summer; www.countyhall gallery.com; charge), displaying 500 works by the Catalan artist, Salvador Dalí. Bear in mind, though, that you can see far more important works by the surrealist artist for free at Tate Modern *(see p.68)*, a little further east along the riverbank.

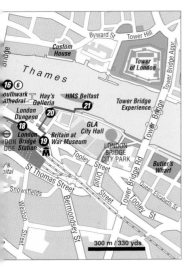

London Aquarium

The top attraction in County Hall, especially for children, is the **London Aquarium** (tel: 020-7967 8000; daily 10am–6pm, last entry 5pm; till 7pm in summer; www.londonaquarium.co.uk; charge). Among the thousands of specimens here, some 350 different species are represented. Highlights include the sharks, a pool where you can touch some of the inhabitants as they surface and, of course, feeding time (Mon, Wed and Fri noon–12.30pm in the Atlantic Tank; shark feeding on Tue, Thur and Sat 2.30pm; times do sometimes change, so call ahead to check).

LONDON EYE

Next stop is the **London Eye ❷** (tel: 0870-990 8883; Oct–May: daily 10am–8pm, Jun–Sept: daily 10am–9pm; www.londoneye.com), the world's largest observation wheel, designed by husband-and-wife architects David Marks and Julia Barfield.

The 32 enclosed capsules take 30 minutes to make a full rotation, which is slow enough to let passengers step in and out of the capsules while the wheel is moving. On a clear day, you can see for 25 miles (40km). Book ahead (by phone or via the website) if you want to ride at busy periods, although, if you can, check the weather forecast first.

SOUTHBANK CENTRE

Now continue along the riverside walk to the brutalist concrete **Southbank Centre ❸** (bookings tel: 0871 663

Above from far left: the London Eye; Shakespeare's Globe; London Aquarium; crossing the Millennium Bridge from Tate Modern to St Paul's Cathedral.

Above: South Bank attractions: Dalí Universe; BFI's Imax cinema; The Clink.

Head for Heights

At 450ft (135m), the London Eye is the fourth tallest structure in London. The hub and spindle weigh 330 tonnes, more than 40 double-decker buses. On average, 10,000 people take a 'flight' on it every day.

Above from far left: browsing the bookstalls in front of BFI Southbank; the Imax.

Iconic Design

As you pass the Hayward Gallery, look out for the neon tower on its roof. Commissioned in 1970 from Philip Vaughan and Roger Dainton for a Kinetics exhibition, this garish London landmark is composed of yellow, magenta, red, green and blue neon strips, which are controlled by changes in the direction and velocity of the wind.

Annual Frost Fair

On the third weekend in December, Bankside holds a fair (with an ice slide, stalls, and free events at the Globe), inspired by the Frost Fairs of centuries past which were held when the Thames froze over.

2500; www. southbankcentre.org.uk), the largest arts complex in Europe. The centre regularly puts on free entertainment, from lunch-time gigs and 'Commuter Jazz' (Fri 5.45–7pm) to talks on poetry and art. It is fronted by a row of restaurants (including Giraffe – a good choice if you have children – as well as Wagamama and Strada), music stores and bookshops.

Music Venues

The **Royal Festival Hall** (www.rfh.org.uk) is the sole survivor of the 1951 Festival of Britain, intended to improve Londoners' morale after the austerity of the post-war years. In 2007, a major renovation of the hall was completed, giving it improved acoustics, better foyer facilities and two new restaurants: Skylon, with views of the river, and the ground-floor **Canteen**, see ⑪①.

Food and Drink 🍴

① CANTEEN

Royal Festival Hall, SE1; tel: 0845-686 1122; daily B, L and D; ££
At the back of the Royal Festival Hall, this restaurant is a useful addition to the renovated venue. It offers good-quality modern British food in the sleek white interior as well as on the heated terrace outside.

② BENUGO BAR & KITCHEN

BFI Southbank, SE1; tel: 020-7401 9000; daily L and D; £–££
The decor at BFI Southbank's main restaurant is self-consciously styled, but the food, which includes freshly made salads, pasta dishes, and sandwiches, is reassuringly down-to-earth. Good place for coffee, too.

Next door are the 917-seat **Queen Elizabeth Hall** for music, dance and public lectures, and the 372-seater **Purcell Room**, for recitals of classical chamber music and world music.

Hayward Gallery

Adjacent, on the upper level of the South Bank Centre complex, is the **Hayward Gallery** (daily 10am–6pm, Fri, Sat till 10pm; www.hayward.org.uk; charge), one of London's most important venues for contemporary art exhibitions. Recent shows have included surveys of the work of Dan Flavin, Antony Gormley, Jacques-Henri Lartigue and Alexander Rodchenko.

The Hayward's ambient, mirrored **Waterloo Sunset Pavilion**, designed by Dan Graham as part of the regeneration of the Southbank, stays open between main exhibitions.

BRITISH FILM INSTITUTE

Next en route are two institutions run by the British Film Institute: BFI Southbank (the expanded, rebranded former National Film Theatre, or 'NFT') and, a five-minute walk south of the river, the London Imax.

BFI Southbank

Adjacent to the Hayward is Britain's leading arthouse cinema since 1952, **BFI Southbank** ❹ (020-7928 3232; www.bfi.org.uk). With three auditoria and an intimate studio cinema, it holds more than 2,400 screenings and events every year, from talks by film stars to silent movies with live accompaniment.

The cinema also houses a research area, a shop, and an excellent 'Mediathèque', where visitors can browse the British Film Institute's archive for free (call ahead to reserve). For a drink before a screening, try the ever-popular Film Café in front of the building, with tables and benches sheltering under Waterloo Bridge, or, for more plush surroundings, visit the BFI's **Benugo Bar & Kitchen**, see ⑪②.

London Imax

Film buffs (and those visiting with children) may want to make a detour to the BFI **London Imax** ❺ (0870-787 2525; www.bfi.org.uk), which rises up from the centre of the roundabout at the southern end of Waterloo Bridge. This huge, cylindrical, glass building houses Britain's largest cinema screen – 66-ft (20-m) high and 85-ft (26-m) wide – together with steeply raked seating.

NATIONAL THEATRE

The final building in this stretch is the **National Theatre** ❻ (020-7452 3400; www.nt-online.org; backstage tours: Mon–Sat, 10.15am, 12.30pm – or 12.15pm on Olivier matinee days – and 5.15pm; charge). Built to designs by Sir Denys Lasdun and opened in 1976, this concrete behemoth houses three theatres: the 1,200-seat Olivier, the 900-seat Lyttelton and the Cottesloe (accessed at the side of the building), a more intimate space with galleries on three sides. For a peek behind the scenes, book a one-hour backstage tour.

OXO TOWER

After the theatres, you will pass **Gabriel's Wharf** ❼, a clutch of restaurants and gift shops, and, close by, the Art Deco OXO **Tower** ❽. Architect Albert Moore had grand ideas for this project: as well as erecting what was to become London's second highest commercial building, he wanted to use electric lights to spell out the product's name. When planning permission was refused, due to an advertising ban, Moore came up with the idea of using three letters – O, X and O – as 10-ft (3-m) high windows looking out north, south, east and

Cheap Seats

The National Theatre's current director, Nicholas Hytner, has had some success in broadening the theatre's appeal by offering some cheaper seats (from £10, including some seats in the stalls) in productions sponsored by Travelex. Book as far ahead as possible to snap up the bargains.

Below: Esa-Pekka Salonen conducts Matthias Goerne at the Royal Festival Hall.

Above from left:
Vinopolis's Wine
Wharf, on Stoney
Street; William
Shakespeare; sign
at Gabriel's Wharf;
remnant of Win-
chester Palace on
Clink Street.

Below: warehouses
below the OXO Tower.

west. Inside the tower are several smart
restaurants, see ⑪③.

TATE MODERN

On emerging from the underpass
beneath Blackfriars Bridge, ahead of
you lies what was once the colossal
Bankside Power Station and is now
Tate Modern ❾, home to the Tate's
international contemporary art collection. This is covered in detail in the Tate
to Tate tour *(see p.68)*. Note that Tate's

collection of British art is housed
upstream, at Tate Britain, *see p.70*.

MILLENNIUM BRIDGE

In front of Tate Modern is the **Millennium Bridge ❿**, a pedestrian link to
St Paul's cathedral *(see p.57)*. When it
was unveiled in 2000, it became the first
new river crossing over the Thames in
central London for almost a century
(since Tower Bridge in 1894). However,
on its opening day, crowds on the bridge
caused it to sway alarmingly, and it had
to close for structural amendments by its
architect, Sir Norman Foster. In 2002, it
reopened without a hint of a wobble.

TUDOR THEATRES

Heading further east, you reach Bankside, one of the South Bank's most
historic areas. The district grew up in
competition with the City opposite,
but by the 16th century had become
a den of vice, famous for brothels,
bear- and bull-baiting pits, prize-fights
and the first playhouses, including the
Globe. Its place in history is assured
owing to its links with playwright
William Shakespeare.

Shakespeare's Globe
A replica of the original (1599) open-
air Globe Theatre, called **Shakespeare's
Globe ⓫**, opened here in 1996 after
years of fund-raising by the inspired
American actor Sam Wanamaker, who
sadly died before its completion. The
thatched roof was the first permitted in
London since the Great Fire of 1666.

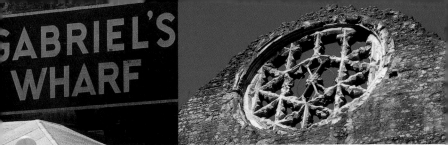

Shakespeare's Globe Exhibition (tel: 020-7902 1500; www.shakespeares-globe.org; May–Sept: daily 9am–noon, Oct–Apr: daily 10am–5pm; charge), to the right of the theatre, fills in the background on the area's historic past. Just opposite is **Tas Pide**, see ⑪④, a good place for a spot of lunch.

The Rose Theatre

Shakespeare's works were also shown at the Rose, Bankside's first playhouse, built in 1587. The **Rose Exhibition** ⑫ (56 Park Street; 10am–5pm, www.rose theatre.org.uk) documents its history.

BANK END AND CLINK STREET

At Bank End is the Anchor pub, where little has changed in over 200 years. Across the street, in the vaults under the railway viaduct, is **Vinopolis** ⑬ (tel: 0870-241 4040; daily noon–6pm; Fri–Mon till 9pm, www.vinopolis. co.uk), which runs informative wine tours with tastings alongside its wine shop and smart restaurant, see ⑪⑤.

The Clink

On **Clink Street** are the surviving fragments of what was once the Bishop of Winchester's 13th-century town residence. The bishops were the first authority in England to lock up miscreants, and their prison operated from 1151 to 1780. The phrase 'in the clink', now a euphemism for being in jail, is thought to stem from the sound made by the clanking chains. The **Clink Street Museum** ⑭ (daily 10am–6pm, www. clink.co.uk; charge) recalls the area's gruesome past.

The Golden Hinde

At the far end of Clink Street is St Mary Overy Dock, where parishioners were once able to land goods free of toll or have their wives put in the ducking stool. A gleaming replica of Sir Francis Drake's diminutive ship the **Golden**

Food and Drink 🍴

③ OXO TOWER
Oxo Tower Wharf, Barge House Street, SE1; tel: 020-7803 3888; daily L and D; £££
Some find it overpriced, but this iconic location is still hugely popular. The biggest draw is the fabulous view of the Thames through huge windows. The food is modern British. A glamorous venue for cocktails, though, sadly, not a cheap one.

④ TAS PIDE
20–2 New Globe Walk, SE1; tel: 020-7633 9777; daily L and D; ££
A local favourite that is also excellent for vegetarians. There is a wide choice of (mostly vegetarian) *meze*, as well as *pide* (Turkish 'pizza') and appealing mains, from grilled sardines to lamb kofta. There are branches also at 72 Borough High Street (tel: 020-7403 7200), towards London Bridge, and 33 The Cut (tel: 020-7926 2111), near Waterloo.

⑤ CANTINA VINOPOLIS
1 Bank End, SE1; tel: 020-7940 8333; daily L and D; ££
Soaring, cathedral-like decor, competently executed modern British food and, not surprisingly, an exceptional wine list (over 150 options) at the restaurant within the wine wharf.

Globe Productions
The season of this open-air theatre runs from May to early October. The theatre can accommodate around 1,500 people – 600 standing (and liable to get wet if it rains) and the rest seated. The wooden benches feel rather hard by Act III, but you can bring or rent cushions. If you have a bargain 'standing' ticket, bring waterproofs, in case of downpours; note that the use of umbrellas is not allowed in the auditorium during performances. If you cannot make it to a show, consider going on one of the tours of the Globe instead.

Did You Know?
Bankside Power Station – now Tate Modern – opened in 1963 but generated electricity for little more than 30 years before being declared redundant.

Above from left:
chillis, the excellent
Roast restaurant
and cheese at Neal's
Yard Dairy, all in
or adjacent to
Borough Market.

Hinde **⑮** (tel: 0870-011 8700; www. goldenhinde.co.uk; daily 10am–dusk; charge) now sits in the dock.

SOUTHWARK CATHEDRAL

Follow the road round to the right and then bear left along the lane and through the gate to **Southwark Cathedral** **⑯** (tel: 020-7367 6700; www. southwark.anglican.org; free). Shakespeare was a parishioner here, and a memorial in the south aisle shows him reclining in front of a frieze showing Bankside during the 16th century; above it is a modern stained-glass window depicting characters from his plays. John Harvard, who gave his name to the American university, was baptised here, and is commemorated in the Harvard Chapel.

Free organ recitals are held at the cathedral on Monday (1.10–1.50pm), while free classical concerts take place on Tuesday (3.15–4pm). The refectory, see ⑪⑥, is a cosy place for refreshment.

BOROUGH MARKET

In the shelter of the cathedral is another of the area's highlights: **Borough Market** **⑰**, a wholesale food market dating back to the 13th century. On Thursday, Friday and Saturday (the last two are the busiest days) a popular retail market offers gourmet and organic products. Apart from staples such as fruit, vegetables, bread and cheese, you will find stalls specialising in game, dried fruits, nuts, oils, vinegars, cakes, preserves, ecologically sound produce, wines and beers.

There are lots of opportunities to sample the produce for free at the market. Many stalls also do takeaway food, from venison burgers to scallops that are pan-fried while you wait. **Tapas Brindisa**, see ⑪⑦, on the south-

---

Food and Drink

⑥ SOUTHWARK CATHEDRAL REFECTORY
Southwark Cathedral, London Bridge, SE1; tel: 020-7407 5740; daily B, L and T; £–££
The restaurant at the back of the cathedral does hearty, well-priced soups and main dishes. The terrace is a bonus in summer. Also open for breakfast, morning coffee and afternoon tea (8.30am–5pm).

⑦ TAPAS BRINDISA
18–20 Southwark Street, SE1; tel: 020-7357 8880; Fri, Sat B, L, D, Mon–Thur L and D; £££
The sleek restaurant connected to one of the most popular stalls in the market is usually packed thanks to its authentic tapas and a buzzing ambience. The only downside is that they do not take reservations.

⑧ ROAST
Floral Hall, Stoney Street, SE1; tel: 020-7940 1300; Mon–Sat B, L, D, Sun D; £££/££££; set meal (Mon–Fri L) ££
In its impressive situation on the upper floor of Borough Market, this restaurant offers fine views through its vast windows. The delicious food, procured from the market, is resolutely British, and includes succulent organic Banham chicken and sturdy game pies. Breakfasts are scrumptious (Mon–Fri till 9.30am, later at weekends) and offer a cunning way to enjoy the upmarket dining experience at a fraction of the cost of lunch or dinner.

western corner of the market, serves high-quality Spanish food. Another excellent option is **Roast**, see ⑪⑧.

TOWARDS TOWER BRIDGE

London Bridge Station, where you could end the tour, is just adjacent. If you still have a spring in your step, continue east, along Tooley Street to nos 28–34, where you can find the **London Dungeon** ⑱ (tel: 020-7403 7221; www.thedungeons.com; Sept–Jun: daily 10am–5.30pm, July, Aug: daily 9.30am–6.30pm; charge). Lasting about $1\frac{1}{2}$ hours, a tour led by actors features ghoulish exhibits on the Black Death, the Great Fire of 1666, Jack the Ripper's exploits, Sweeney Todd the barber's gruesome deeds, a boat ride to hell, in which visitors pass through Traitors' Gate before being condemned at court, and Extremis, a white-knuckle ride.

It is fun for kids who like the macabre, but the entire visit is spent in darkened corridors, so it is not recommended for children under eight. Even under-15s must be accompanied by an adult. Queues can be long, so book in advance if you can. Tickets are expensive.

Next door is **Winston Churchill's Britain at War Museum** ⑲ (www. britainatwar.co.uk; Oct–Mar: 10am–5pm, Apr–Sept: 10am–6pm, last entry 1 hour before closing; charge), which recreates the atmosphere of the Blitz.

Hay's Galleria
Now cross over the road to the old Hay's Wharf. In the 19th century, tea clippers from India and China docked here; now filled in, the wharf has been renamed **Hay's Galleria** ⑳, and operates as a smart atrium of shops, including an independent bookstore, several clothes shops, a branch of Boot's, and a couple of restaurants. Look out for David Kemp's water sculpture *The Navigators* in the middle of the yard, and the nearby *boules* pitch.

HMS Belfast to Tower Bridge
To continue the walk further still, head east along the river, where you cannot miss the World War II cruiser *HMS Belfast* ㉑ (tel: 020-7940 6300; daily 10am–6pm, www.hmsbelfast.org.uk; charge). Its tour takes in the engine rooms, the cramped accommodation of its 950 crew and archive film footage.

From here, if you continue east you will reach Tower Bridge, where you could cross the bridge to link up with tour 9 *(see p.55)*. Alternatively, return to London Bridge for the tube.

Above from left: Hay's Galleria; Southwark Cathedral; cheese-seller at Borough Market; Tower Bridge raised to let a large vessel through.

Super Snug
On the corner of Winchester Walk and Stoney Street, look out for the tiny Rake pub, which is reportedly the smallest one in London.

Local Watering Holes

Not known historically for its sobriety, Southwark still has many pubs. The George Inn (77 Borough High Street), mentioned by Charles Dickens in *Little Dorrit* and now owned by the National Trust, is London's only galleried coaching inn. The Market Porter (9 Stoney Street) is famous for opening its doors from 6–8.30am for Borough Market workers. The riverfront Anchor (34 Park Street) has stood on this site for some 800 years and was a haunt of diarist Samuel Pepys and, later, Dr Samuel Johnson.

THE GEORGE

TATE TO TATE

Visit Tate Modern, now London's no. 1 tourist attraction, and one of the world's most innovative modern art museums, then speed up the river on a catamaran to Tate Britain for a survey of British art through the centuries.

Peregrine Falcons
During recent summers, when not chasing their lunch through the air, peregrine falcons have roosted on the 99-m (325-ft) high chimney of Tate Modern. Bird conservationists set up their telescopes below, so that members of the public can get a good view.

DISTANCE 2¼ miles (3.5km) not incl. distance covered in galleries
TIME A full day
START Tate Modern, Southwark
END Tate Britain, Pimlico
POINTS TO NOTE
We suggest booking your boat trip on arrival at Tate Modern, so that you can spend the morning at Bankside, take the boat to Pimlico, have lunch, then spend the afternoon at Tate Britain. Alternatively, combine this tour with walk 10, covering the South Bank.

There are now two Tate galleries in London, and two outside, in Liverpool and St Ives. The original foundation for the gallery was laid by Henry Tate (who made a fortune by inventing the sugar lump); it opened in 1897 as a department of the National Gallery. The collection now also encompasses the national holdings of international modern and contemporary art.

TATE MODERN

The route begins on the south bank of the river at **Tate Modern ❶** (tel: 020-7887 8888; www.tate.org.uk; Sun–Thur 10am–6pm, Fri–Sat 10am–10pm; free except special exhibitions). The nearest tube stations are London Bridge or Southwark (south of the river) and Blackfriars (north of the Thames), all about 10 minutes' walk away. The lamp-posts between Southwark tube station and the gallery are painted orange to show visitors the way.

The Building

In 1998, the Tate made the bold decision to purchase the disused Bankside Power Station, and Swiss architects Herzog & de Meuron won the competition to transform it into an art gallery. The industrial character of Sir Giles Gilbert Scott's original brick structure

(built in two stages between 1947 and 1963) was retained. They saved the vast Turbine Hall for housing large-scale art installations, reopened the block's monumental windows and fitted a light at the top of the huge central chimney.

The Collection

The permanent collection at Tate Modern is displayed in four suites, over two floors (levels 3 and 5), and focuses on definitive moments in 20th-century art history: Surrealism, Minimalism, post-war Abstraction, and the three linked movements of Cubism, Futurism and Vorticism. The galleries on level 4 stage temporary exhibitions, often of international importance. Note also the restaurant on level 7, see ⑪①.

Level 3

On level 3 is 'Material Gestures', using post-war abstract European and American painting and sculpture as a focal point, with precursors and successors traced alongside. The works of Barnett Newman and Anish Kapoor are shown together, as are paintings by Claude Monet and Mark Rothko. Abstract Expressionism is displayed in the context of earlier figurative expressionism. Worth a quiet moment is the room devoted to Rothko's sombre *Seagram Murals* (1958–9), commissioned for a restaurant in the Seagram Building on Park Avenue, New York. It is not hard to see why Rothko decided they would sit better in a less commercial setting.

Next, 'Poetry and Dream' focuses on Surrealism, embracing the diverse range of techniques and styles of Miró,

Ernst, Dalí, Magritte, Klee and Man Ray. Their influence is then pursued to Picasso and Pollock, Francis Bacon and Joseph Beuys, Cindy Sherman and Gillian Wearing, as well as to cinema, periodicals, and performance art.

Level 5

This level begins with 'Idea and Object', examining the reaction away from the subjective, expressionistic, painterly art of the post-war period. Instead, objectivity and impersonality are embraced, with all the associated ideas of Minimalism, Conceptualism, Utopianism and the shifting status of artists and viewers. Look out here for Carl Andre's pile of bricks (1966), Marcel Duchamp's toilet urinal, *Fountain* (1917) and Andy Warhol's Brillo boxes (1964).

Finally comes 'States of Flux', devoted to Cubism, Futurism and Vorticism. Alongside classic statements of these approaches – by Braque, Picasso, Boccioni and Wyndham Lewis – their influence is shown cropping up in various quarters, from the graphic design of Stalinist Russia to the collages of Pop Art.

Above from far left: artist Damien Hirst and Tate Director Nicholas Serota with Hirst's *Mother and Child Divided 2007* in 'Turner Prize: A Retrospective' at Tate Britain; view from Tate Modern over the Thames and the Millennium Bridge to St Paul's; studying the artworks at Tate Modern; the Turbine Hall.

The Turbine Hall
This vast hall is five storeys tall, with 37,000 sq ft (3,400 sq m) of floor space, and is used for specially commissioned work by contemporary artists. In 2000, it was Louise Bourgeois's huge spider sculpture, *Maman, I Do, I Undo, I Redo*. In 2003, Olafur Eliasson created *The Weather Project*, with a mirror sky, sun and mist. Then in 2006, Carsten Höller built *Test Site*, comprising spiralling slides, allowing visitors to whiz down the full height of the hall. In 2007, Doris Salcedo created *Shibboleth*, consisting of a crack running through the the concrete floor.

RIVER

Above from left:
John Everett Millais's
Ophelia (1851–2),
a highlight of Tate
Britain's 2007/8
special exhibition
'Millais' and also its
permanent collection;
sign for the river boat.

Turner Prize
The country's most
prestigious and
controversial annual art
prize is usually hosted
at Tate Britain. Many
criticise the judges'
predilection for
conceptual artists,
such as Tracey Emin,
who in 1999
submitted her own
double bed or Richard
Deacon, whose *For
Those Who Have Eyes*
(1983) is shown
above. In 2002, culture
minister Kim Howells
left feedback at the
exhibition of shortlisted
artists: 'if this is the
best British artists can
produce then British
art is lost,' and
followed this up with a
choice expletive while
decrying conceptual
artists' 'lack of
conviction'. Others,
however, credit the
prize with raising the
profile of British art.

TATE BOAT

The **Tate Boat** runs every forty minutes during gallery opening hours, shuttling back and forth between Tate Britain and Tate Modern, and stopping off at the London Eye along the way.

Tickets are available from Tate Modern and Tate Britain, as well as online and by calling 020-7887 8888, or, subject to availability, on the boat itself.

Embarking from the small pier in front of Tate Modern, you are taken in the 220-seat catamaran (with exterior and interior designs by artist Damien Hirst) to Millbank pier in front of Tate Britain. This new pier has been designed by the architects David Marks and Julia Barfield, who also designed the London Eye. It also features a lighting installation by artist

Angela Bulloch, who was shortlisted for the 1997 Turner Prize. Fluorescent tubing embedded into the floor of the pontoon is computer programmed to provide changing lighting effects on the structure at night.

TATE BRITAIN

Tate Britain ❷ (Millbank; tel: 020-7887 8000; www.tate.org.uk; daily 10am–5.50pm; free except special exhibitions) in Pimlico is the original Tate Gallery and home to the national collection of British art from 1500 to the present day. Opened in 1897, it was designed by Sydney Smith in classical style, and built on the site of a prison.

The permanent collection is almost entirely contained on one floor (level 2) and is organised roughly chronologically. As you enter the building through the front porticoed entrance on Millbank, you go through a succession of grand halls with galleries off to the left and right.

Art from 1350 to 1800
Walking beyond the octagon to the hall at the back you will find on your left Room 1, where the chronology begins. Here are English alabaster sculptures from *c.*1350–1450, and in the next room, Tudor and Stuart portraits. Look out for Nicholas Hilliard's portrait (*c.*1575) of Queen Elizabeth I in one of her bejewelled dresses.

The next few rooms take you through the 17th and 18th centuries, with glamorous portraits by Van Dyck, social satire by Hogarth, and aristo-

---

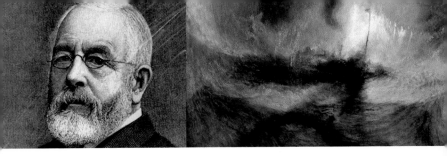

cratic portraits and allegorical scenes in the Grand Manner by painters including Gainsborough, Reynolds, and one of the few women artists of the time, Angelica Kauffman.

Romanticism and Victorian Art

Rooms 7 to 11 are devoted to the transition from a classicising to romantic aesthetic. This is most explicit in the depiction of the natural world. The landscape painting of John Constable is well represented here, while the seascapes of J.M.W. Turner have their own dedicated (east) wing of the museum, the Clore Gallery *(see below)*.

The following rooms are rich in Victorian genre painting, with its narrative content and obsessive period detail. Also here are the Pre-Raphaelites who created sharply realistic paintings in pure,

brilliant colours. Millais's romantic *Ophelia* (1851–2) is one of the gallery's most popular pictures.

Modern Art

On the east side of the gallery are rooms devoted to 20th-century British art. As well as discernible movements such as Vorticism and Pop Art, and groups such as those from Camden Town and St Ives, there are also modern masters who do not fit so easily into categories: Stanley Spencer, Francis Bacon and Lucian Freud among them.

When you have finished your survey of British art, retire to the restaurant downstairs ⑪②, or else head for the dependable **Grumbles**, see ⑪③, just off Belgrave Road to the north of Pimlico tube station.

Above from centre: Henry Tate; Turner's spectacular *Snow Storm: Steam-Boat off a Harbour's Mouth.*

Late at the Tate On the first Friday of each month, Tate Britain stays open until 10pm, and exhibition entry is half-price. There is also an excellent programme of performances, music, talks and films, though these tend to be very popular, so arrive early to queue for the free tickets.

Turner Bequest

On his death in 1851, London-born (in Covent Garden's Maiden Lane, where a blue plaque commemorates the fact) Joseph Mallord William Turner (1775–1851) left a large sum of money and his collection of 20,000 paintings and drawings to the British nation, expressing the wish that a special gallery be built to house them all together. It took until 1987 for this to happen, when the Clore Gallery designed by the British architect James Stirling was opened beside Tate Britain. Even now, however, some of his paintings are scattered across other collections, contrary to his wishes. Masterpieces on display include *Peace – Burial at Sea*, showing the artist's mastery in depicting light as affected by objects, rather than the other way round, and *Snow Storm: Steam-Boat off a Harbour's Mouth*, suggestive of Turner's fascination with the elemental forces of nature. In order to paint the sensational effect achieved in the latter, Turner tells us in his subtitle that 'The Author was in this Storm on the Night the *Ariel* left Harwich', lashed, at his own request, to the ship's mast.

HYDE PARK

On May Day 1660, Samuel Pepys wrote in his diary, 'It being a very pleasant day I wished myself in Hyde Park.' Three and a half centuries later, in the heart of a much-changed London, people still feel exactly the same way.

Speakers' Corner

People have been congregating in the north-east corner of the park to air their views since the 18th century. Before that, it was the location of the Tyburn hanging tree, where executions had taken place since the 12th century. The right of public assembly here was formalised in law in 1872 following the Reform League's large rallies in 1866 and 1867 in support of the right of working-class men to vote. Famous speakers here have included Karl Marx, Friedrich Engels, Vladimir Lenin, William Morris, George Orwell and the Pankhursts. Over a million people, the largest turn-out in its history, protested here in 2003 against the Iraq War.

Upside-Down Tree

Near the rose gardens is the Weeping Beech, *Fagus sylvatica pendula*, cherished as 'the upside-down tree'.

DISTANCE 2¾ miles (4.5km)
TIME Half a day
START Apsley House
END Queensway tube
POINTS TO NOTE

People with restricted mobility can book an electric buggy, driven by a volunteer (tel: 07767 498096; May–Oct: Tue–Fri 10am–5pm).

Hyde Park was first opened to the public in 1637 by Charles I. It had previously been a deer park used by Henry VIII for hunting and, before that, a manor owned by Westminster Abbey since before the Norman Conquest.

The adjacent Kensington Gardens was sectioned off as the grounds of Kensington Palace in 1689, when William III moved here from White-hall Palace. Today, all 625 acres (253 ha) of the park are once again open to the public.

Food and Drink 🍴

① THE DELL CAFÉ

South side of the Serpentine; tel: 020-7706 7098; daily, summer 9am–8pm, winter 9am–4pm; £–££
Pavilion with terrace overlooking the Serpentine for summer dining. Serves simple meals and snacks.

APSLEY HOUSE

The route begins at **Apsley House ❶** (tel: 020-7499 5676; Tue–Sun Apr–Oct 10am–5pm, Nov–Mar 10am–4pm; charge), near Exit 1 of Hyde Park Corner tube station. Once known as No. 1 London, since it was the first house encountered after passing the tollgates of Knightsbridge, this was where the Duke of Wellington lived from 1817 until his death in 1852, and part of the house is still home to his descendants today.

The house was designed by the architect Robert Adam and built between 1771 and 1778. On its passing to the Duke of Wellington, the house had its original brick exterior faced with stone, and the portico and columns were added. Inside, however, much of the original Adam design survives, including the staircase, drawing room and portico room.

Following the Duke's victory at Waterloo, gratitude was heaped upon him from various quarters in the form of plate and porcelain, paintings, sculpture and chandeliers. The art collection includes works by Goya, Rubens, Correggio and Brueghel. One gift he should perhaps have refused is a 11-ft (3.4-m) high nude statue of Napoleon that dominates the stairwell.

HYDE PARK

Enter **Hyde Park ❷** (tel: 020-7298
2100; www.royalparks.org.uk; daily
5am–midnight; free) via the **Triumphal
Screen** to the left of Apsley House.
This monumental entrance was commissioned from Decimus Burton by
King George IV in the 1820s along with
the Wellington Arch, which was later
moved to the middle of the roundabout.

If you are fortunate to be here in
mid-morning, you might wait at this
point to see the Household Cavalry
who emerge from their barracks at
10.30am every morning (9.30am on
Sunday) on South Carriage Drive and
ride across the park to Horse Guards
Parade for the changing of the guard.
The other road (unmetalled) running
east–west and converging on Hyde
Park Corner is **Rotten Row** – a cor-
ruption of Route du Roi – the king's
route from Kensington Palace to
Westminster. It was the first road in

England to be lit at night – by 300 oil
lamps. The Crystal Palace, the spectacular iron-and-glass showcase of the
1851 Great Exhibition, once stood
between the two roads. (It was moved
after the exhibition to Sydenham Hill,
in south-east London, but sadly burnt
down in 1936.)

The Serpentine

Now take the Serpentine Road north-
west, past the bandstand on your right,
and the rose gardens on your left, to
the northern bank of the **Serpentine
❸**. This lake was created by Queen
Caroline in 1730 by damming the river
Westbourne. It achieved notoriety in
December 1816 when the pregnant
wife of the poet Shelley committed
suicide by plunging into the icy waters;
Shelley married Mary Wollstonecraft
Godwin two weeks later. Today, the
lake has its own swimming club and
is scene of a famous Christmas Day
100-yard race (tel: 020 7706 3422;

Above from far left:
leafy Hyde Park;
Speakers' Corner.

Below: commem-
orative wreaths;
Household Cavalry by
Hyde Park.

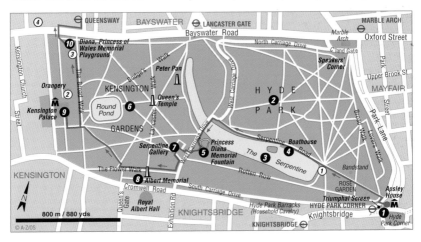

www.serpentine lido.com), when the foolhardy take to the chilly waters.

On your left as you come to the lake is the **Dell Café**, see ⑪① *(p.72)* and further round is the **Boathouse** ④, where, from March to October, you can rent rowing boats and pedalos, or take a trip on the solar-powered ferry boat.

Continuing, you reach the boundary between Hyde Park and Kensington Gardens at West Carriage Drive. Turn left, past the **Powder Magazine** (originally for storing gunpowder), and cross the bridge that was designed by John Rennie in 1826.

To the left of the road on the other side of the bridge is the **Princess Diana Memorial Fountain** ⑤, designed by the American architect Kathryn Gustafson. This innovative fountain has, unfortunately, been dogged by controversy since opening in 2004, owing to the initial cost (£3.6m), and the heavy burdens of ongoing maintenance and supervision.

Skating

Each December Hyde Park hosts an ice-skating rink. In the summer, rollerbladers meet en masse at the bandstand (every Wed 7.30pm).

Queen's Temple

Walk north-west from the Serpentine Gallery to find Queen Caroline's Temple on your right (built 1734–5 by William Kent). Further up is a statue, *Physical Energy* by G.F. Watts (1907).

Food and Drink 🍴

② THE ORANGERY
Kensington Gardens; tel: 020-7166 6112; daily B and L 10am–6pm, till 5pm in winter; £–££
Light lunches and afternoon tea. Outside seating in summer.

③ BROADWALK CAFÉ
Kensington Gardens; tel: 020-7034 0722; daily, summer B, L and D, 8am–8pm, winter B and L 10am–4pm; £
Ideal for children. Serves salads, pizzas, fruit, yoghurts, ice creams.

④ CAFÉ DIANA
5 Wellington Terrace, Bayswater Road; tel: 020-7792 9606; daily B, L and early D 10am–6pm; £–££
The walls are plastered with photos of the princess. Serves wide variety of snacks as well as all-day breakfasts and some Middle Eastern dishes.

KENSINGTON GARDENS

Cross over West Carriage Drive and you enter **Kensington Gardens** ⑥ (tel: 020-7298 2141; www.royalparks.org.uk; daily 6am–dusk; free). You might have been denied the pleasure of access had Queen Caroline (wife of George II) had her way. On enquiring of Prime Minister Walpole what the cost might be of reclaiming the, by then, public gardens for her private use, she received the reply, 'Only a Crown, Madam'.

Serpentine Gallery

Follow the path off the road for the **Serpentine Gallery** ⑦ (tel: 020-7402 6075; www.serpentinegallery.org.uk; daily 10am–6pm; free). This classical-style 1934 tea pavilion puts on major exhibitions of modern and contemporary art. Every spring, a leading architect (Daniel Libeskind, Rem Koolhaas, etc), is commissioned to build a temporary pavilion (June–Sept) alongside.

Albert Memorial

Now follow the signposts along the south-westerly path for the **Albert Memorial** ⑧, commissioned by Queen Victoria in memory of her beloved husband, Prince Albert, who died of typhoid in 1861. This Gothic-revival monument was designed by Sir George Gilbert Scott and unveiled in 1872. It centres around a gilded Albert holding a catalogue of the Great Exhibition of 1851. He is surrounded by massive representations of the continents and sits enshrined in a white marble frieze depicting 187 poets and painters. The

180-ft (55-m) spire is inlaid with semi-precious stones.

Across the road to the south is the **Royal Albert Hall** (tel: 020-7589 3203; www.royalalberthall.com), opened in 1871, and now the venue for concerts, including the Proms every summer.

Kensington Palace

Next, to reach **Kensington Palace ❾** (tel: 020-7937 9561; www.hrp.org.uk; daily Mar–Oct: 10am–6pm, Nov–Feb: 10am–5pm; charge), continue west, and take a path off to your right in a north-westerly direction. The house came into royal hands in 1689, when William III bought it in the hope that the country air would alleviate his asthma. Additions were made at this time by Sir Christopher Wren, and later by William Kent for George I. Since then it has been inhabited by various members of the Royal Family, most notably Princess Diana, who lived here until her death in 1997. Today it is the official residence of Prince and Princess Michael of Kent among others.

Highlights inside include the Ceremonial Dress Collection, which has 14 dresses worn by Princess Diana as well as lavish costumes worn for state occasions. Also impressive is the King's staircase, with its wall paintings by William Kent of George I's court: look out for the King's Polish page Ulric, the Turkish servants Mahomet and Mustapha, Peter 'the wild boy' – a feral child found in the woods in Germany – and a portrait of the artist himself, with his mistress at his shoulder, looking down from the ceiling.

The Palace Gardens

Outside the Palace, just to the east, near the path by which you entered, is the sunken Dutch garden, and, on the other side of the path, a statue of Queen Victoria sculpted by her daughter, Princess Louise, to celebrate 50 years of her mother's reign.

North is Hawksmoor's **Orangery**, where Queen Anne liked to take tea, and you can too, see ⑪②. Beyond that is the **Diana, Princess of Wales Memorial Playground ❿**, where children can make up for having been so well behaved in the tea room. And when they are tired from clambering over the huge pirate ship at the playground's centre, there is another café for ice creams and cakes, see ⑪③.

Finally, in the north-west corner of the park, leave by the Orme Square Gate, which after 5pm (4pm in winter) is the only exit open. On Bayswater Road, turn right for Queensway tube or left for **Café Diana**, see ⑪④.

Peter Pan

Walk north from the Serpentine Gallery and in a leafy glade by the Long Water is a statue of Peter Pan. It was here that the Llewelyn Davies children, who inspired the Peter Pan stories, were brought to play by the author J.M. Barrie (he had become co-guardian after their parents died). In one story, Peter Pan flies out of his nursery and lands beside the Long Water, on the spot where the statue now stands. The sculpture was made by Sir George Frampton and put up in the middle of the night of 1 May 1912 to surprise children playing in the park the next day.

SOUTH KENSINGTON AND KNIGHTSBRIDGE

Museums of decorative arts, natural history and science – the Victorians' rich legacy – are the improving highlights of this tour, after which you can make a rather less edifying visit, to Harrods, London's most famous corner shop.

Crystal Palace

Joseph Paxton's design for a crystal palace was a late entry in the competition to find a suitable structure in which to house the Great Exhibition. Paxton was in fact not a professionally trained architect at all, but instead the former gardener to the Duke of Devonshire.

DISTANCE 1¼ miles (2km) not incl. distance covered in museums
TIME A full day
START South Kensington tube
END Knightsbridge (Harrods)
POINTS TO NOTE

All three of the museums described are vast, and visiting all of them in one day would be exhausting; instead, concentrate on one or two, according to interest. Entrance to each is, however, free, meaning that popping in to see one or two prize exhibits in each is perfectly feasible.

The year 1851 is remembered in Britain for the Great Exhibition, held in Hyde Park in a glass-and-metal palace designed by Joseph Paxton. Aspects of the far-flung Victorian Empire were brought under the curious gaze of a public whose interest in the sciences and the arts had seemingly never been greater. The idea for the exhibition came from Henry Cole (1808–82), chairman of the Society of Arts, and it was taken up enthusiastically by the royal consort Prince Albert, who chaired the committee to see it through. The resultant Crystal Palace built in the park was a great success, with more than 6 million visitors; after it moved to Sydenham, southeast London, the following year, the profits were used to purchase 87 acres (35ha) of land in adjoining South Kensington to build a more permanent home for the arts and sciences. The area is the focal point of this tour.

V&A

Start at **South Kensington tube station**, where a good pitstop for an unusual lunch is **Daquise**, see ①①. When you are ready to head on to the museums, take the underpass in the

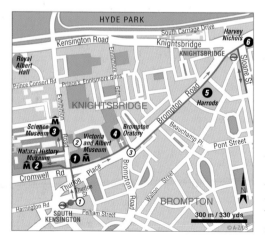

tube station signposted 'Museums', which brings you out on Cromwell Road, right by the **Victoria and Albert Museum** ❶ (tel: 020-7942 2000; www.vam.ac.uk; daily 10am–5.45pm, Wed till 10pm; free).

The Foyer

The museum is vast, with around 5 million objects in its collection, stored in roughly 8 miles (13km) of corridors. Start in the main foyer, where you can admire the Venetian-style 'chandelier' by American glass artist Dale Chihuly. The spectacular accretion of blue, green and yellow glass was erected in 1999 as a talking-point for the Victorian foyer, and was doubled in size in 2001 to a height of (33ft) 10m. It was assembled *in situ* by a team of technicians, each piece of glass slotted over an angled rod.

Lower Ground and Ground Floors

On the ground floor, located on the right of the entrance, are the **Sculpture Courts**, which house British and European Neoclassical works from the late 18th and early 19th centuries. To the left of the entrance (past the main shop) are the vast *Raphael Cartoons* (1515–6), on loan from the Queen. These drawings, depicting scenes from the lives of St Peter and St Paul, were commissioned by Pope Leo X as templates for a series of tapestries in the Sistine Chapel.

Opposite the *Raphael Cartoons* is a section on costume, while above this (a staircase leads straight upstairs) is the museum's collection of musical instruments. Adjacent, on the ground floor,

is the Asian and Islamic collection, where highlights include spectacular rugs and carpets and the extraordinary *Tipu's Tiger*, a carved automaton of an Indian tiger killing a British officer, made *c*.1790 for Sultan Tipu.

Flanking the great courtyard are rooms containing the Italian Collection, and, at the end of this section, near the Ceramic Staircase (which symbolises the symbiotic relationship between art and science), are the three original refreshment rooms, where first-, second- and third-class menus were served prior to World War II. Allusions to food and drink are worked into the decoration. The room by Arts and Crafts pioneers William Morris, Philip Webb and Edward Burne-Jones is particularly fine.

Upper Floors

Upstairs, most galleries focus on materials or techniques, such as silver, ironwork (home to Sir George Gilbert Scott's intricate 1862 Hereford Screen), stained glass, ceramics (the whole of the top floor), textiles and jewellery. The **British Galleries**, documenting British taste from 1500 to 1900, are also here.

Above from far left: V&A entrance; Prince Albert; imposing glass staircase at the V&A; *Tipu's Tiger*.

Below: 16th-century Iranian Ardabil carpet; Dale Chihuly's 'chandelier' in the foyer.

Late Opening

Henry Cole began assembling the V&A collection the year after the Great Exhibition, but Queen Victoria did not lay the foundation stone of the current building until 1899, 38 years after Albert's death.

Food and Drink 🍴

① DAQUISE

20 Thurloe Street; tel: 020-7589 6117; daily 11.30am–11pm; Mon–Fri set lunch; ££
Reach this Polish restaurant by taking the right-hand exit out of South Kensington tube, and turning immediately right. Daquise is at the end of the row of shops. A loyal Polish and local clientele come here for the excellent authentic food at very cheap prices (especially for this upmarket area). The decor, including the squishy banquettes, has not changed for decades.

Above from left: the Natural History Museum's main hall and escalator up to a globe and the entrance to the Earth Galleries.

Terrible Lizards
On the landing of the Natural History Museum, overlooking the main hall, is a statue of Richard Owen, the museum's first director. He was the first to recognise the existence of giant prehistoric land reptiles and called them dinosaurs ('terrible lizards').

Below: the Natural History Museum's cavernous main hall.

Henry Cole Wing

The last remaining section is the Henry Cole Wing, spread over six floors and devoted mostly to changing exhibitions of prints, drawings, paintings and photographs. Also here is the **Frank Lloyd Wright Room**, transplanted here from Pittsburgh and the only example of the architect's work in Europe. End the tour here with a visit to the museum's café, see ⑪②.

NATURAL HISTORY MUSEUM

Across Exhibition Road is the neo-Gothic **Natural History Museum** ❷ (Cromwell Road; tel: 020-7942 5000; www.nhm.ac.uk; daily 10am–5.50pm; free). The collection was originally a department of the British Museum, but by the mid-19th century had outgrown the available space and in 1881 the present museum opened; it now shelters around 75 million plants, animals, fossils, rocks and minerals.

Life Galleries

The first half of the museum is classed as the 'Life Galleries', although ironically its chief attractions – the dinosaurs – are well and truly dead. Just past the information desks, in the middle of the Central Hall, is the cast of a diplodocus unearthed in Wyoming in 1899. At 26m (85ft), it is the longest complete dinosaur skeleton ever discovered.

The **Dinosaur Gallery** is one of the busiest sections of the museum, and many visitors make a bee-line for the robotic dinosaurs at the far end. The full-scale animatronic **T-Rex** on long-term loan from Japan is responsive to human movement; the roaring, life-like model twists and turns, delighting most children (and frightening some).

Human Biology examines the workings behind the human body, from hormones to genes, and is packed with interactive exhibits: test your memory or be tricked by optical illusions.

The spectacular suspension of a life-sized blue whale model is the highlight of the **Mammals** section. As well as displaying an astonishing array of taxidermy, these galleries contain sobering statistics on the rate at which species are becoming extinct.

The gallery of **Fish, Amphibians and Reptiles** highlights fascinating species, including fish that live well

between the sea's twilight zone at 400m (1,300ft) and total darkness at 1,000m (3,300ft). Next door is the contrastingly serene **Marine Invertebrates**, where cabinets of corals, shells and sea fans are enhanced by the sound of waves breaking on a shore.

Earth Galleries

Head through Waterhouse Way towards the museum's other main section: the Earth Galleries. This section is brought to life by exciting special effects and atmospheric sound and lighting. A central escalator transports visitors into a gigantic rotating globe. At the top, **Restless Surface** includes highly imaginative coverage of earthquakes and volcanoes: the tremors of an earthquake are simulated in a mock-up of a Japanese mini-market; a bank of TV sets next to a car covered in volcanic ash replays news reports of the 1991 eruption of Mt Pinatubo in the Philippines.

In **From the Beginning**, the story of the universe is told, from the time of the Big Bang 15,000 million years ago to the end of the solar system, which is pencilled in for 5,000 million years from now. Finally, demonstrating the sheer beauty our planet has to offer, is the **Earth's Treasury** gallery, which displays rocks, gems and minerals glittering in semi-darkness.

SCIENCE MUSEUM

Just around the corner on Exhibition Road is the third museum developed after the success of the 1851 Great Exhibition, the **Science Museum** ❸ (tel: 0870-870 4771; www.science museum.org.uk; daily 10am–6pm; free). This museum traces the history of inventions from the first steam train to the space rocket and has over 10,000 exhibits, plus such additional attractions as an Imax theatre.

Ground Floor

The museum's ground floor is home to **Exploring Space** and **Making the Modern World**. The former's highlight is a replica of the *Apollo 11* lunar excursion module, but its scope covers videos of early rocket experiments in the 1920s.

Making the Modern World (with 'modern' defined as post-1750) brings together many of the museum's prize exhibits. Here you can find the world's oldest surviving steam locomotive, *Puffing Billy* (*c*.1815), Stephenson's pioneering *Rocket* passenger locomotive (1829) and the battered *Apollo 10* command module (1969).

Third Floor

Head up to the third floor for the magnificent **Flight Gallery**, with exhibits ranging from a seaplane to a Spitfire

Above: attractions at the Science Museum include: the Energy Hall, dominated by a 1903 mill engine; the Making of the Modern World, with a Lockheed Electra airliner hanging in silvery splendour from the ceiling; and the Exploring Space gallery, with a huge Spacelab 2 x-ray telescope – as used on the Space Shuttle.

Food and Drink

② **V&A CAFE**

Victoria and Albert Museum, Cromwell Road; tel: 020-7942 2000; daily 10am–5.15pm, Fri till 9.30pm; £–££
Characterfully set in the vaults of the V&A's cellars and now run by the successful Benugo chain, the main museum restaurant does pastries for breakfast, excellent soups with crusty bread, fresh, modern salads, delicious cakes, and is licensed. In summer there is also a cafe for drinks and snacks in the garden court.

to hot-air balloons. The 1919 Vickers Vimy, in which Alcock & Brown made the first non-stop transatlantic flight, is here, as is a Messerschmitt rocket-propelled fighter and the first British jet aircraft, the Gloster Whittle E28/39. Visitors can peer into the cockpit of a Douglas DC3 and participate in interactive exhibits illustrating the principles of flight. A flight simulator offers a rodeo-style ride (charge).

Now go back downstairs to the basement. As well as a child-orientated area, it houses the **Secret Life of the Home**, a collection of domestic appliances and gadgets that provoke nostalgia in adults and disbelief in children. A range of models charts the development of the electric toaster since 1923. Other everyday items include a 1925 Sol hairdryer and a 1945 Goblin Teasmade.

Other exhibits that are geared more towards adults include **Energy: Fuelling the Future**, **Health Matters**, **Glimpses of Medical History** and **Psychology: Mind Your Head**, while the games of **In Future** raise intriguing questions for everyone. Meanwhile, the **SimEx Simulator** (charge) creates the sensory effect of things such as having a dinosaur breathing down your neck, through air and motion manipulation.

Harrods' Motto

The store boasts that it can find any item you could want and then send it anywhere in the world, with the motto 'Everything for Everyone Everywhere'. Under this remarkable policy, Noël Coward was bought an alligator for Christmas, former US president Ronald Reagan was given a baby elephant, and highly unusual items, such as your very own wax model by Madame Tussauds, can be made a reality (albeit with the rather hefty price tag of around £250,000).

KNIGHTSBRIDGE

End the route by walking east along Cromwell Road, which then turns into the Brompton Road. Note, on your left, **Brompton Oratory** ❹ (Thurloe Place; tel: 020-7808 0900; www.brompton oratory.com; daily 6.30am–8pm; free), a flamboyant Italian Baroque church designed by 29-year-old architect Herbert Gribble. Opposite is a good option for a French meal, **Racine**, see ⑪③.

Harrods and Around

Head up Brompton Road towards Knightsbridge tube station and, at nos 87–135, the department store **Harrods** ❺ (tel: 020-7730 1234; Mon–Sat 10am–8pm, Sun noon–6pm). East End grocer Henry Charles Harrod opened a store here in 1849, in anticipation of trade sparked by the Great Exhibition. The Harrod family sold the company in 1889, but the store still flourished. Construction of the current building, by C.W. Stephens, architect of Claridge's hotel, started in 1901. The Egyptian Al Fayed brothers bought the store in 1983.

Highlights include the magnificent Art Nouveau food hall, a good place to buy provisions for a picnic in nearby Hyde Park *(see p.72)*, just north of Knightsbridge and South Carriage Drive. Alternatively, if you want to finish the tour with some shopping, continue east on Knightsbridge to the upmarket **Harvey Nichols** ❻ department store, or walk south down Sloane Street, which is lined with designer names and leads to the King's Road and Chelsea *(see opposite)*.

Food and Drink 🍴

③ RACINE
239 Brompton Road; tel: 020-7584 4477; daily L and D; £££
The smart glass exterior promises a sophisticated meal, and you will not be disappointed by the classic French fare cooked with panache. It is great value for this part of town, especially the three-course set menu, available till 7.30pm.

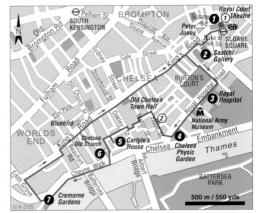

CHELSEA

A Wednesday or Sunday afternoon visit to London's oldest garden and the homes of many famous writers, with a glimpse of sunset on the Thames and a walk along one of the capital's most famous shopping streets.

Riverside Chelsea was little more than a fishing village until around the 15th century, when it became fashionable with aristocrats who built smart country houses along what was then the private royal route linking Westminster with the palace of Hampton Court to the west: the King's Road.

In the 19th and 20th centuries the area drew artists enticed by the riverside setting and quality of the light. The 1960s marked the peak of its fame, but in the 1980s the area still had some edge, reflected by the opening of Vivienne Westwood and Malcolm McLaren's cult shop, Sex, at no. 430 King's Road.

Although Westwood's shop, renamed World's End (the name of the part of Chelsea west of the kink in the King's Road) is still there, the area is now far from cutting-edge; instead, it is one of the smartest, and most expensive, parts of London, and the domain of the wealthy 'Sloane Ranger' *(see right)*.

SLOANE SQUARE

Start by the tube, on the eastern side of **Sloane Square ❶**, laid out in the late 18th century and named after Sir Hans Sloane, a wealthy physician and collector who purchased the manor of Chelsea in 1712. To your right is the **Royal Court** (bookings tel: 020-7565

> **DISTANCE** 3¾ miles (6km)
> **TIME** Half to a full day
> **START/END** Sloane Square
> **POINTS TO NOTE**
> Do the walk on a Wednesday or Sunday if you want to go into the Chelsea Physic Garden, as it only opens on those days. Saturdays are very busy on the King's Road.

5000; www.royalcourttheatre.com), dating from 1870. This is where John Osborne's mould-breaking *Look Back in Anger* was first staged in 1956, and it still has a reputation for good new material. If you want a pitstop, the café here, see ⑪① *(p.82)*, is an excellent choice.

Above from far left:
Harrods by night;
Chelsea Pensioners.

Sloane Rangers
Commonly used since the 1960s, this term for the stereotypical preppie young Chelsea inhabitant became official in 1982, when society magazine *Harpers & Queen* published *The Official Sloane Ranger Handbook*.

Walk along the south side of the square. Note to your right the department store, **Peter Jones** (part of the John Lewis chain), whose architects managed the transition from square to street in a sensuous curve.

DUKE OF YORK SQUARE

Continue west on the King's Road. On your left is Duke of York Square, a pedestrian enclave of upmarket homeware and fashion units, cafés and, in winter, an ice rink. Partridges the grocers organises a regular Saturday food market outside their shop. Behind is the Duke of York's Headquarters, formerly a military campus. Since 2008 it has housed the **Saatchi Gallery** ❷ (visit www. saatchi-gallery.co.uk for information; charge), showcasing the work of contemporary British artists collected by former advertising mogul Charles Saatchi and noted for its collection of works by the YBAs (Young British Artists) such as Damien Hirst and Tracey Emin.

ROYAL HOSPITAL

Back on the King's Road, you must resist the temptation to shop in its many fashion and shoe stores and take the next left, Cheltenham Terrace. At the end, continue on to Franklin's Row, which hits Royal Hospital Road.

In front of you is Chelsea's **Royal Hospital** ❸ (tel: 020-7881 5200; www. chelsea-pensioners.org.uk; Mon–Sat 10am–noon and 2–4pm, May–Sept also Sun 2–4pm; free), a grand building, inspired by the Hôtel des Invalides in Paris and built by Christopher Wren in 1692. This is home to approximately 400 Chelsea Pensioners, retired war veterans who are identifiable by their red uniform coats. Next to the hospital is the **National Army Museum** (tel: 020-7881 2455; daily 10am–5.30pm; free).

CHELSEA PHYSIC GARDEN

Continue west along Royal Hospital Road until you reach no. 66 and the **Chelsea Physic Garden** ❹ (tel: 020-7352 5646; www.chelseaphysicgarden. co.uk; Apr–Oct: Wed noon–5pm, Sun 2–6pm; charge); the entrance is on the left, on Swan Walk. Founded by the Society of Apothecaries in 1676, it is second only to the one in Oxford as the oldest botanic garden in the country, with thousands of rare and unusual plants, including the largest outdoor olive tree in Britain. The themed trails for children and adults are fun.

CARLYLE'S HOUSE

At the end of Royal Hospital Road you hit Flood Street, where you should turn right for the excellent **Coopers Arms**, see ⑪②; Margaret and Denis Thatcher once lived on this street, at no. 19. From the pub, go west through the area's network of pretty streets – along Alpha Place, over Chelsea Manor Street on to Oakley Gardens, then west on Phene Street and Upper Cheyne Row – to Cheyne Row itself.

At no. 24 time stands still in **Carlyle's House** ❺ (tel: 020-7352 7087; www.nationaltrust.org.uk; mid-Mar–end Oct: Wed–Fri 2–5pm, Sat, Sun 11am–5pm; charge). The Scottish historian Thomas Carlyle brought his wife Jane to live here, in this elegant Queen Anne house, in 1834.

Their home was turned into a museum in 1896 and remains a time capsule of Victorian life, with papered-over panelling and books, furniture and pictures just as the Carlyles left them. What the 'Sage of Chelsea' did not find was peace and quiet. His sound-proof attic study, built on the roof, failed to keep out the noise of cocks crowing, street musicians and horses' hooves.

CHEYNE WALK

At the north end of Cheyne Row turn left into Upper Cheyne Row and Lawrence Street, home of the Chelsea porcelain works from 1745–84. Dr Johnson fancied his hand at the wheel, but his pots never survived the firing. Continue on to Cheyne Walk, one of London's most exclusive streets. Past residents include George Eliot, J.M.W. Turner and Dante Gabriel Rossetti *(see right)* and, more recently, Mick Jagger.

Here, you will be confronted by a lumpen, gilded statue of Sir Thomas More, another famous resident. Henry VIII's chancellor went to the Tower, and was beheaded in 1535, having prepared his resting place in **Chelsea Old Church** ❻. The building was nearly destroyed by a land mine in 1941 but was reassembled from the shattered fragments. Highlights include two carved capitals by Holbein.

Cremorne Gardens

On your left at this point, note the houseboats that are moored by Battersea Bridge. The riverside walk here is attractive, but the road turns away from the river at **Cremorne Gardens** ❼, a secluded spot where Victorians danced the night away beneath the coloured lanterns.

BACK TO SLOANE SQUARE

Edith Grove on the right will take you back to the King's Road. A brisk 25-minute walk (not including stops) past its shops will take you back to Sloane Square; alternatively, catch bus nos. 11 or 22 heading east. As you head back to the square, look out, on your left, for Terence Conran's renovated Bluebird Garage, at no. 350, and, on the right, halfway along the King's Road, the Old Chelsea Town Hall, a popular spot for celebrity marriages. Flanking the town hall are two antiques markets.

Above: gourmet quiches at the Duke of York's market; bedding and velvet slippers at Designers Guild.

ROUTEMASTER BUS TRIP

Take your furled brolly and Bowler hat and hop on the no. 15 from the Tower of London to Trafalgar Square, via St Paul's Cathedral. 'All aboard for Ludgate Circus!' shouts the conductor. Ding ding. And the bus trundles off…

End of an Era

The iconic 'Routemaster' double-decker bus was introduced in London in 1956 and remained in general service until 2005. However, owing to Government legislation requiring full accessibility to public transport for wheelchair users by 2017, only two 'Heritage' routes, the no. 9 and no. 15, still use Routemasters.

DISTANCE 2¾ miles (4.5 km)

TIME 25 minutes

START Tower Hill

END Trafalgar Square

POINTS TO NOTE

The no. 15 bus is scheduled to take 25 minutes to complete its route but can take longer in rush hour, running daily every 15 minutes 9.30am–6.30pm in both directions. Note that not every no. 15 is a Routemaster, so wait until one arrives for this tour. The other 'Heritage' route, the no. 9, continues from Trafalgar Square to the Albert Hall, via Piccadilly Circus, Hyde Park Corner and Knightsbridge. Conductors accept Travelcards, Oystercards or cash fares.

If you arrive by tube, turn right as you leave Tower Hill station, towards the Tower of London. Cross the road via the subway and ascend the steps to your left for the bus stop. This may be a good time to visit the Tower of London *(see p.55)* before catching the no. 15.

TOWARDS EASTCHEAP

Once on the bus, on your right is the grand **Port of London Authority building** ❶. Then on your left, just past the Tower of London is **All Hallows Church** ❷, the City's oldest, dating from 675. Next, driving up Great Tower Street, on your right, up Mincing Lane, you glimpse **The Gherkin** ❸, Norman Foster's peculiarly shaped office tower.

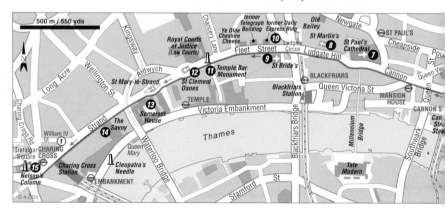

TOWARDS OLD BAILEY

As the street becomes Eastcheap, ('east market' – it was lined with butchers' stalls in medieval times), on the right is Sir Christopher Wren's **Church of St Margaret Pattens** ❹. Soon after, on the left is **Pudding Lane**, where the Great Fire of 1666 *(see p.20)* began in a bakery; it is commemorated by the column of **The Monument** ❺ *(see p. 56)*. The bus then crosses King William Street, which leads left to **London Bridge**, and right towards the Bank of England and, in the distance, the **Barbican Tower**.

Now on Cannon Street, to your right is Wren's **St Stephen Walbrook** ❻ and rising up behind, the 1970s' **Tower 42** (the old NatWest Tower), once Britain's tallest skyscraper. Next – and unmissable – on the right is **St Paul's Cathedral** ❼, while a glance to the left reveals the Millennium Bridge over the river to **Tate Modern**. Moving on to Ludgate Hill, on the right, is **St Martin's Church** ❽, and beyond, the **Old Bailey**, the scene of many famous criminal trials.

FLEET STREET AND STRAND

Past Ludgate Circus on to Fleet Street, you will see **St Bride's Church** ❾, which inspired the tiered wedding cake, on the left, down Bride Lane. On the right are the black Art Deco former newspaper offices of the **Daily Express** ❿ (nicknamed 'Black Lubyanka') and, shortly afterwards, at no. 135, those of **The Telegraph**. Next on the right is **Ye Olde Cheshire Cheese**, one of the City's oldest pubs, followed by the **Law Courts** towards the end of Fleet Street.

The start of the Strand is marked by the dragon of the **Temple Bar monument** ⓫, set in the middle of the road, and soon afterwards, Wren's **St Clement Danes** ⓬, the church of the Royal Air Force. Then, to the left of the other island church, **St Mary-le-Strand**, is **Somerset House** ⓭, now a major art museum *(see p.54)*. Shortly afterwards on the same side of the road is the **Savoy Hotel** ⓮, which was built by Richard D'Oyly Carte, who also produced Gilbert and Sullivan operas.

Finally, the bus rolls into **Trafalgar Square** ⓯, where the tour ends. After your bumpy ride, repair to the **Tappit Hen**, see Ⓨ①, for a traditional lunch.

Above from far left: Routemaster buses at the depot; on the top deck.

Wren Churches
In the 16th century, there were 111 churches in the City of London; the Great Fire of 1666 destroyed 87 of them. Sir Christopher Wren was appointed King's Surveyor of Works and directed the rebuilding of 51 churches, including St Paul's Cathedral. Today, 23 of these remain almost intact, while ruins or only towers of a further six also survive, and the rest have either been entirely destroyed (several in the Blitz) or substantially rebuilt.

Food and Drink
① THE TAPPIT HEN
5 William IV Street, Strand; tel: 020-7836 9839; Mon–Fri 9am–11pm; ale and porter house downstairs: lunch only; ££
As the name suggests (a Tappit Hen is a triple-sized bottle of wine), this wine bar is a good place for a boozy lunch with traditional British food: Scottish herrings, bangers and mash, lamb shank, treacle tart, cheeseboard; also freshly cut sandwiches. Candlelit tables and sawdust floors in the ale house downstairs.

HAMPSTEAD

Full of pretty houses on leafy groves and set against the backdrop of its glorious heath, Hampstead seems the quintessence of an English village. In reality, it is not so much rural idyll as exclusive suburb, a haven in a hectic city.

Freud Museum

Walk south on Heath Street and Fitzjohn's Avenue, turn right at Nutley Terrace and left on to Maresfield Gardens for Sigmund Freud's house (tel: 020-7435 2002; Wed–Sun noon–5pm; charge). All is just as the psycho-analyst left it, including his couch.

DISTANCE 2¾ miles (4.5km)
TIME Half a day
START/END Hampstead tube
POINTS TO NOTE
The best days to walk this route are Thursday, Friday and Saturday, when all the museums are open. Also, try to pick a sunny day, when walking on the heath is most agreeable. Note that Kenwood House is about 15–20 minutes' walk from Hampstead tube.

Until not so long ago, Hampstead was the home of artists, writers and anyone with a liberal disposition. At the last count, the suburb had over 90 blue plaques commemorating such famous residents as John Constable, George Orwell, Florence Nightingale and Sigmund Freud. Now, you only need to have deep pockets to live here: its pretty alleys, leafy streets and fine heath make this villagey suburb a desirable address.

From **Hampstead tube station**, take Heath Street south (past **The Horseshoe**, see ⑪①) and turn right at Church Row, a street of Georgian houses. Follow the sign to John Constable's grave in the bosky graveyard of **St John's Church ①**, halfway down.

FENTON HOUSE

Now head north up Holly Walk, past the one-time home of Scottish writer Robert Louis Stevenson, and turn left up to Hampstead Grove. On your left is **Fenton House ②** (Windmill Hill; tel: 020-7435 3471; Mar: Sat, Sun 11am–5pm, Apr–Oct: Wed–Fri 2–5pm, Sat, Sun 11am–5pm; charge), a grand William-and-Mary mansion built for a merchant. Behind the gilded gates, the walled garden, with its apple orchard and rose garden, has hardly changed for 300 years. Inside are fine paintings, fur-

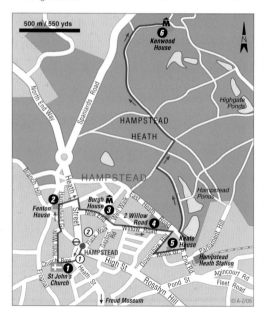

niture, porcelain and a collection of harpsichords. In spring, concerts here recreate 18th-century parlour parties.

BURGH HOUSE

Back on Hampstead Grove, turn right and descend the steps back to Heath Street, then cross over to New End. At the far end of the street is New End Square and **Burgh House** ❸ (tel: 020-7431 0144; Wed–Fri and Sun noon–5pm; free). Built in 1704, it contains the local history museum, with a permanent display on painter John Constable and maps showing the location of 166 homes of celebrated residents.

Almost opposite the museum is the turning for Flask Walk, a pleasant detour taking you past boutiques and galleries to **The Flask**, see ⑪②.

WILLOW ROAD

Returning to New End, continue on to Willow Road. At the far end, overlooking the heath, is the Modernist **2 Willow Road** ❹ (tel: 020-7435 6166; Apr–Oct: Thur–Sat noon–5pm, Mar and Nov: Sat only; charge), designed by Erno Goldfinger (after whom the James Bond baddie was named) for himself. Inside is his art collection, with works by Henry Moore, Bridget Riley, Max Ernst and Marcel Duchamp.

KEATS HOUSE

Next turn right on Downshire Hill, and then left on to Keats Grove. On the right is **Keats House** ❺ (tel: 020-7435

2062; closed for refurbishment until late 2008, then Tue–Sun 1–5pm; charge), the Regency villa where the consumptive poet lodged before departing for Rome, where he died a year later, in 1821, aged 25. Under a plum tree in the garden he penned one of his best-loved poems, *Ode to a Nightingale*. Inside are his keepsakes of Fanny Brawne, the neighbour with whom he fell in love.

HAMPSTEAD HEATH

At the end of Keats Grove, turn left on to South End Road and take one of the paths on your right on to the heath. The heath is criss-crossed with paths, but bear north for the top of the hill and **Kenwood House** ❻ (tel: 020-8348 1286; daily Apr–Oct 11am–5pm, Nov–Mar 11am–4pm; free). This mansion was bequeathed to the nation by brewing magnate, Edward Guinness, and houses his art collection, with works by Rembrandt, Vermeer, Reynolds and Turner. It also contains some of Robert Adam's finest interiors (from 1764 –79).

Outside again, stroll through the gardens and the heath beyond to return to Hampstead tube station.

Above from far left: the view from Hampstead Heath; Keats remembered.

Spaniards Inn
At the northern end of Spaniards Road is this 16th-century coaching inn, where highwayman Dick Turpin used to stable his horse, Black Bess, while noting which carriages to hold up later. It was also here that the poet Keats heard the nightingale that inspired his famous ode.

Highgate Ponds
Among the Heath's attractions are its open-air ponds, with single-sex, mixed and nude areas. There is also a 196-ft (60-m) long lido (tel: 020-7485 5757) at Parliament Hill. With this in mind, it is worth taking your swimming costume on this tour if the weather is good.

Food and Drink

① THE HORSESHOE
28 Heath Street; tel: 020-7431 7206; daily L and D; ££–£££
Good real ales (the pub has its own microbrewery). Classic British food: lamb and beef dishes, then trifle or fruit crumble and custard.

② THE FLASK
14 Flask Walk; tel: 020-7435 4580; Mon–Sat L and D, Sun L; ££
Typical Victorian pub: comfortable and with two bars at the front separated by a fine 1880s glazed partition. Standard pub food.

NOTTING HILL

Notting Hill's appeal derives from its fusion of cultures and lifestyles – Rasta meets pasta, bourgeois splendour combines with bohemian chic. The best time to come is on a Saturday when Portobello Road market is in full swing.

What's in a Name?

Before *c*.1850, Portobello Road was a country lane snaking through hayfields and orchards. Its name derives from that of a nearby pig farm, which in turn was named after an English victory over Spain at Puerto Bello in the Gulf of Mexico in 1739.

DISTANCE 2 miles (3km)
TIME Half a day
START Notting Hill Gate tube
END Westbourne Park tube
POINTS TO NOTE

The Saturday market on Portobello Road gets extremely crowded by mid-morning, so arrive very early to snap up the bargains. There are also some stalls on Fridays and Sundays. If, on reaching Westway flyover, you want to escape the throng, Ladbroke Grove tube station is off to the left.

Notting Hill became fashionable in the 1990s, when monied people from the worlds of fashion and media moved in, attracted by the lingering street cred of the mix of ethnic cultures and shabby chic look. The neighbourhood is now extremely expensive and largely the province of investment bankers.

Go back in time, however, and it is a very different story. In the 1800s, when the area's grand crescents sat next to noxious slums, it was, according to Dickens, 'a plague spot scarcely equalled for its insalubrity by any other in London'. As recently as the 1950s, the district was very poor. Large numbers of Afro-Caribbean immigrants settled in overcrowded lodging houses, and the area saw race riots in 1958.

Now different cultures rub along more happily, though the local population has become largely white middle class, and the famous Notting Hill Carnival has grown from modest beginnings in the 1960s to be the world's second largest after the one in Rio.

PORTOBELLO ROAD

Leaving **Notting Hil Gate tube station**, turn right (north) off Notting Hill Gate on to Pembridge Road. Walk past the retro shops and turn left into Portobello Road. The top part of the road

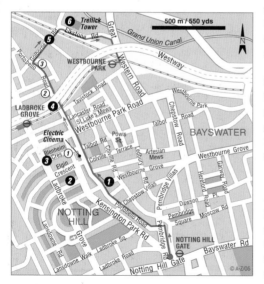

is largely residential, with pretty terraces painted different colours. Look out for the blue plaque at no. 22, where the writer George Orwell used to live.

Street Market

Further down, beyond the turning for **Westbourne Grove ❶**, you enter the thick of the market for antiques and collectables. Dozens of stalls are hidden away in arcades such as the Admiral Vernon, on your left. Many are open only on Saturdays, when the streets are thronged with vendors hawking toast racks and teddy bears, plant pots and Ming vases. Bargaining is expected.

At the turning for **Elgin Crescent ❷**, the theme changes to food, with traditional greengrocery sitting side by side with organic olive bread. Behind stalls of pak choi and ciabatta, on your left at no. 191, is the **Electric Cinema** (tel: 020-7908 9696; www.the-electric. co.uk), which screens current films in a vintage setting, with leather armchairs, footrests and wine coolers.

Further up, turn left down **Blenheim Crescent ❸** for **Books for Cooks**, see ⑪①, and, opposite, the Travel Bookshop. The latter was the inspiration for the bookshop in the 1999 film, *Notting Hill*, starring Julia Roberts and Hugh Grant; the film was criticised locally for all but air-brushing out the area's Afro-Caribbean inhabitants.

Beyond the Westway

Back on Portobello Road, walk under the concrete of the **Westway flyover ❹**, where the market becomes a showcase for boho fashion. Boutiques in Portobello Green Arcade sell pink heart-shaped sunglasses and fake fur gilets, while stalls outside sell vintage clothes, old LPs and retro design.

Towards Golborne Road

If you are in need of a pitstop, **Uncle's**, see ⑪②, is on your left, and, at the end of Portobello, there is the **Galicia**, see ⑪③. You are now near the junction with **Golborne Road ❺**, where you should turn right. Here, Moroccan shops sell slippers and spices, and the Portuguese community queues for coffee and cakes at the Lisboa (no. 57) and dried salt cod, *bacalao,* at the deli opposite. At the end of the road looms **Trellick Tower ❻**, designed by Erno Goldfinger, after whom James Bond's old adversary was named. Turn right on Elkstone Road for the tube station.

Food and Drink 🍽

① BOOKS FOR COOKS
4 Blenheim Crescent; tel: 020-7221 1992; Tue–Sat 10am–6pm; £–££
This shop devoted to cookery books also offers cookery classes and the opportunity to sample the (usually excellent) results in its small cafe.

② UNCLE'S
305 Portobello Road; tel: 020-8962 0090; daily B, L and D; £–££
Informal café where you can read the newspaper and eat breakfast at any time of day. Nice big fat chips.

③ THE GALICIA
323 Portobello Road; tel: 020-8969 3539; daily L and D; ££
Chaotic tapas bar and restaurant serving the local Spanish community. Tasty, unpretentious, authentic dishes.

Above from far left: colourful Portobello Road; antiques on Kensington Church Street; well-loved bear in a local shop; Notting Hill Carnival.

Carnival

On the August bank holiday each year, the streets of Notting Hill are packed with around a million people celebrating the massive three-day Caribbean festival. The first carnival, a small affair, was held in St Pancras Town Hall in 1959 to unite communities after race riots; it moved to Notting Hill in 1965. The main carnival days are the Sunday and Monday, though visit on Saturday night and you can hear the steel bands practise.

Below: Notting Hill and Portobello Road are popular among the fashionista crowd.

THE EAST END

Where once were slums, race riots and Jack the Ripper are now art galleries, trendy bars and gritty urban cool, while Canary Wharf, once the docks of Britain's imperial trade, is the power–architecture of investment banks.

Women's Library

Turn right as you leave Aldgate East Tube for the turning for Old Castle Street and the Women's Library (tel: 020-7320 2222; Tue–Fri 9.30am–5pm, Sat 10am–4pm; free). Converted from a Victorian bathhouse, it documents the history of women's rights, suffrage and sexuality.

DISTANCE 2½ miles (4km)
TIME A full day
START Whitechapel Art Gallery
END Geffrye Museum
POINTS TO NOTE
To attend the markets in full swing at Petticoat Lane, Spitalfields or Columbia Road, walk this route on a Sunday. Note also the very limited opening times of Dennis Severs' House *(see opposite)*.

Long associated with poverty, over-crowding and inner-city grime, the increasingly gentrified East End is now under the spotlight as the location of the 2012 Olympic Games, to be held in Stratford. As well as being home to its indigenous cockneys, the area has historically also been the first stopping-point for immigrants in London and hosts a wide range of ethnicities. Its cultural mix, edgy atmosphere and once-cheap accommodation have also made it popular with artists in the last few decades. Meanwhile, over in the Docklands, it is the investment bankers who have moved in, housed in sky-scrapers and posh riverside apartments on the former docks, once so vital to Britain's imperial trade.

WHITECHAPEL

From Aldgate East tube station, follow the signs to the exit next to the **Whitechapel Art Gallery ❶** (tel: 020-7522 7888; www.whitechapel.org; Wed–Sun 11am–6pm, Thur till 9pm; free). The gallery was founded by a local vicar and his wife in 1897 who aimed to combat spiritual and economic poverty in the East End, and the building was designed by the Arts and Crafts archi-tect Charles Harrison Townsend. Today, it mounts high-quality exhibitions of

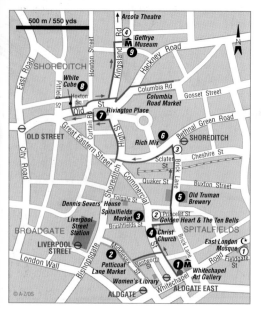

contemporary art. There is also an excellent café on the mezzanine level.

Leaving the gallery, turn right along Whitechapel Road to continue the route, or, if ready for lunch, turn left towards the **East London Mosque**, where Fieldgate Street, on your right, has some of London's best Pakistani restaurants, including 🍴①.

SPITALFIELDS

London's Old Markets

Just west of the Whitechapel Gallery, turn into Commercial Street on your right. Heading north, off to your left down Wentworth Street is **Petticoat Lane Market ❷** (Mon–Fri and then greatly expanded on Sun until 2pm), a centre of the rag trade for 400 years.

Further up Commercial Street, on your left, is **Spitalfields Market ❸**, formerly London's wholesale fruit-and-vegetable market (since 1682), and now hosting stalls selling fashions, jewellery, homewares, second-hand books and organic food stalls on Sundays.

Eating and Drinking

On the other side of the road is **The Golden Heart** pub, renowned for being popular with the BritArt crowd – the indulgent and eccentric landlady, Sandra Esquilant, was recently voted the 80th most important person in the contemporary art world. The ghost of the Quaker prison reformer Elizabeth Fry is supposed to turn off beer taps in the cellar from time to time. A few doors along is **St John**, see 🍴②, and a little further still, on the corner of

Fournier Street, is **The Ten Bells** pub, where Jack the Ripper eyed up his victims before murdering them.

Christ Church Spitalfields

On the other corner of Fournier Street is **Christ Church ❹** (tel: 020-7247 7202; Mon–Fri 11am–4pm, Sun 1–4pm; free), one of Nicholas Hawksmoor's finest works. It was built from 1714 to 1729 to underline the power of the Church of England to the dissenting Huguenots who had settled in the area after fleeing Catholic France.

Walking down Fournier Street you pass the fine houses the Huguenots built once they had grown wealthy from silk weaving and silver smithing.

Brick Lane – 'The Curry Mile'

At the end of the street, turn left on to Brick Lane, famous for its cheap curry

---

Food and Drink 🍴

① TAYYABS

83 Fieldgate Street; tel: 020-7247 9543; daily L and D; £
Chaotic, often long queues, but good food (and prices). Delicious Seekh kebabs – succulent and tasty. Bring your own alcohol (no corkage).

② ST JOHN BREAD AND WINE

94–6 Commercial Street; tel: 020-7251 0848; B, L and D daily; £££
Offshoot of the St John restaurant in Smithfields. Follows the same successful recipe, though slightly cheaper. Menus change daily, offering fresh British produce using chef Fergus Henderson's concept of nose-to-tail eating. Native oysters, pig's head and radishes, smoked eel and pickled prunes, fennel and Berkswell.

---

18 Folgate Street
Two streets beyond Spitalfields Market is the 18th-century time warp of Dennis Severs' House (tel: 020-7247 4013; www.dennissevers house.co.uk; 1st and 3rd Sun of the month noon–4pm, Mon following first and third Sun of month noon–2pm, no booking; Mon nights by candlelight, booking; charge). In 1967, Severs moved from his native California and bought this silk weaver's house. Living with no electricity or modern appliances, he recreated its 18th-century state. It is now as if the original family have just left the room, leaving a half-eaten scone and a smouldering fire.

Flower Market
On Sundays between 8am and 2pm, Columbia Road is taken over by a flower market. Have a mooch, bide your time in a café and at the end of the session the remaining plants and flowers are sold off cheaply.

Top from left:
local girls; spices and poppadums – this part of town is famous for its Indian restaurants; seamstress on Brick Lane, reflecting the increasingly creative slant of the area and its connections with the rag trade.

Right: period room in the Geffrye Museum.

houses, thanks to another immigrant community, this time the Bangladeshis.

Crossing Brick Lane is Princelet Street, with its fine early 18th-century houses intact *(see right)*. Further up is the **Old Truman Brewery** ❺, which houses shops, studios, bars, restaurants (including the excellent Story Deli), nightclubs, and, on Sundays, a craft market. Towards the end of the street, among the boutiques and cafés of this now-fashionable area is a relic of its once sizeable Jewish community – **Beigel Bake**, see ⑪③, on your left.

HOXTON AND SHOREDITCH

At the top of Brick Lane, turn left on to Bethnal Green Road. On your right is **Rich Mix** ❻ (tel: 020-7613 7490; www.richmix.org.uk; daily 9am–11pm), a former garment factory, which now houses a cinema, art galleries and

recording studios. Just beyond is the crossroads with Shoreditch High Street, where you turn right.

This area was very heavily bombed during World War II, and suffered severe depopulation thereafter – by 1960, St Leonard's Church on the High Street had no parishoners left. Regeneration only took root in the 1990s, when artists moved in attracted by the cheap studio space. With their success, galleries, bars and nightclubs followed – and higher prices.

Rivington Place
Located on your left, just off the High Street, is Rivington Street, with, on your right, London's newest public gallery, **Rivington Place** ❼ (tel: 020-7749 1240; www.rivingtonplace.org; Tue–Sat 11am–6pm, Thur till 9pm; charge). Devoted to cultural diversity, the building plays host to art exhibitions and

---

Food and Drink 🍴
③ BRICK LANE BEIGEL BAKE
159 Brick Lane; tel: 020-7729 0616; 24 hours daily; £
Perfect plump, soft beigels. Fillings of smoked salmon, cream cheese, herring, or, best of all, salt beef carved off the joint in front of you. Nice with mustard and gherkins. Also onion platzels, chollah bread, and stupendous cakes. All very cheap. Cheery staff. Better than its competitor a few doors along.

④ SÔNG QUÊ
134 Kingsland Road; tel: 020-7613 3222; L and D daily; £
Vietnamese restaurant with a menu like a phone directory (there are 28 types of noodle soup, for example). Fresh, aromatic food. Friendly service.

film screenings. Its latticed façade was inspired by a Sowei tribal mask.

Hoxton Square

At the end of Rivington Street, turn right on to Curtain Road and left on to Old Street. The first turning on your right is for Hoxton Square. It was here that playwright Ben Jonson killed Gabriel Spencer in a duel in 1598. Today it is a focus of the contemporary art scene in the East End and a fashionable nightlife spot. Immediately on your left is **White Cube ❽** (tel: 020-7930 5373; www.whitecube.com; Tue–Sat 10am–6pm; free), the art gallery that sells the work of Damien Hirst, Tracey Emin and the Chapman brothers.

A detour off the square to the left, past **Sh!**, a boudoir-style women-only sex shop, brings you to Pitfield Street. At no. 17 is **Bookartbookshop**, selling limited-edition artists' books, while at no. 45 is a relic of tatty old Hoxton: **Charlie Wright's International Bar** (tel: 020-7490 8345; daily till the small hours), where the eponymous former weight lifter presides over his dive of a bar where, in the evenings, you can listen to jazz or dance to '80s tracks.

Geffrye Museum

Returning to Old Street, head east, and at the crossroads turn left on to Kingsland Road. (On Sundays go straight on for the Flower Market on **Columbia Road**, the first right turning off Hackney Road – *see left*.) Further up Kingsland Road, on your right is the **Geffrye Museum ❾** (tel: 020-7739 9893; www.geffrye-museum.org.uk;

Tue–Sat 10am–5pm, Sun noon–5pm; free). Housed in a square of former almshouses, built in 1714, this interior-decoration museum first opened in 1914 as a resource and inspiration for workers in the East End furniture trade. It is set up as a series of period rooms taking you from 1600 to the present day. There is also a series of 'period gardens' outside.

Almost next door is the best of the area's many Vietnamese restaurants, see ⑪④. For evening entertainment, take a bus further up Kingsland Road for, on your left, the **Vortex Jazz Club** (tel: 020-7993 3643; www. vortexjazz.co.uk) and, on Arcola Street off to the right, the fringe-style **Arcola Theatre** (tel: 020-7503 1646; www.arcolatheatre.com).

19 Princelet Street

This unrestored 18th-century house was built by Huguenot master silk weavers. In the 19th century it was occupied by Polish Jews, who built a synagogue in the garden. Since the house is in a fragile state, it is only open occasionally. Call 020-7247 5352 for details, or check the website at www.19princeletstreet.org.uk. When the building is stabilised, it is hoped that it will house a Museum of Immigration and Diversity.

The Docklands

From c.1700, London's docks grew as the hub of Britain's imperial trade. In the 1960s, however, their demise came quickly, as trade moved to deep-water ports required for the new container shipping. By 1980, all London's docks were closed, leaving behind derelict land, unemployment and poverty. The 1990s brought regeneration, with the building of the capital's second major financial district, the Canary Wharf complex. Its main tower is Britain's tallest building, at 244m (800ft). Take a ride on the Docklands Light Railway (DLR) from Bank to Greenwich to get an idea of the mix of old and new, rich and poor, then visit the Museum in Docklands at West India Quay or even Mudchute City Farm on Pier Street.

GREENWICH

Compared to central London, Greenwich has a stately but sedate feel. With buildings by Sir Christopher Wren and Inigo Jones, the royal park and a majestic river frontage, it evokes the full splendour of British maritime history.

St Alfege Church
On the site at which St Alfege, an Archbishop of Canterbury, was killed by a raiding party of Danes in 1012, is this church, built by architect Nicholas Hawksmoor in 1714. Inside are memorials to General Wolfe and the composer Thomas Tallis.

DISTANCE 2 miles (3km)
TIME A full day
START *Cutty Sark*
END Greenwich Park
POINTS TO NOTE

To reach Greenwich, take a boat from any of the central London piers, the Docklands Light Railway (DLR) to Cutty Sark station or mainline trains from London Bridge. Note that the full market is held at weekends only.

Of the various ways to get to Greenwich, you could take a boat, just as Queen Elizabeth I used to do, in her state barge rowed from Whitehall to her palace here. The boat today drops you off by the *Cutty Sark* clipper, the starting point for this tour. The DLR *(see grey box left)* also deposits you on the quayside here. If you take the train, however, the *Cutty Sark* is five minutes' walk away – turn left on to Greenwich High Road and follow the road round as it veers left at St Alfege Church. The *Cutty Sark* soon comes into view, ahead and to your right.

ALONG THE RIVER

The Cutty Sark

The **Cutty Sark** ❶ was a clipper that transported tea from China and, later, wool from Australia. Launched in Scotland in 1869, she was the last and fastest of these ships and finally retired in 1922. The ship's name comes from Robert Burns' poem, *Tam O'Shanter*, in which Tam meets a group of witches, all of whom are ugly, but for one, who is young and beautiful and wears only a 'cutty sark' – a short chemise or shirt; the ship's figurehead represents this witch. Unfortunately, while undergoing restoration in 2007, the ship was badly damaged by fire, and at the time

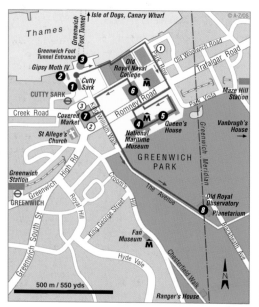

of printing it was not yet known when it would be reopened to the public.

Gipsy Moth IV

Nearby, and dwarfed by the *Cutty Sark* in size, though not in terms of achievement, is another boat, **Gipsy Moth IV** ❷. It was in this ketch that Sir Francis Chichester became the first person to sail solo around the world in 1966–7. It took him 226 days to complete the journey of 29,630 miles (47,685km).

Greenwich Foot Tunnel

Also on the riverfront is the round pavilion containing the entrance to the **Greenwich Foot Tunnel** ❸ (daily dawn–dusk; free). The tunnel was completed in 1902 and allowed south London residents to work in the docks on the Isle of Dogs on the other (north) side of the river. Inside, a lift and a long spiral staircase take you down 50ft (15m) to the tunnel lined with 200,000 glazed white tiles.

River Path

Now walk east along the river path past the two blocks of the **Royal Naval College**. The gap between ensured that the Queen's House (to your right) had unobstructed views of the river. For similarly excellent views of the Thames, refuel at the **Trafalgar Tavern**, see ⑪①.

MARITIME MUSEUM

From Park Row, take a right turn at Romney Road and cross over to the **National Maritime Museum** ❹ (tel: 020-8858 4422; www.nmm.ac.uk; Sept–June: daily 10am– 5pm, Jul–Aug: daily 10am–6pm; free). The museum is formed from the Queen's House and two wings, joined by colonnades.

In the west wing is the main collection, with sections on naval history, polar exploration, colonialism and oceanography. Highlights include the Royal Barge of 1732, decorated with lions, dragons and monsters; and the Nelson

Food and Drink 🍴
① TRAFALGAR TAVERN
6 Park Row; tel: 020-8858 2909; daily L and D; ££
Historic pub built in 1837 where Victorian politicians including Gladstone and Disraeli used to celebrate the end of the parliamentary session with fish dinners. It was also popular with writers Thackeray, Wilkie Collins and Dickens, who set the wedding breakfast scene in *Our Mutual Friend* here. Tissot memorably painted the huge bow windows looking over the river. Renowned for its baskets of whitebait, the more usual pub grub of fish and chips or sausage and mash is also reasonable.

Above from far left: the symmetry of the Royal Naval College and Queen's House from the river; roof of the Covered Market.

Below: stained-glass window, St Alfege; anchor on a pub sign.

Millennium Dome North-east of Greenwich is Britain's monument to the new millennium: a marquee-like structure in the shape of a convex watchface. From the outset the Dome was plagued by controversy, from its initial £750 million construction budget, numerous overspends and government bail-outs, to its unclear function and meagre 25-year lifespan. It has since been renamed the O2 Arena and is now used as a venue for pop concerts.

Left: looking out of the chapel of the Old Royal Naval College.

Above from left:
Greenwich Park; Old Royal Naval College 'Painted Hall' ceiling and chapel ceiling; Vanbrugh's house.

Fan Museum
At 12 Crooms Hill on the western edge of Greenwich Park is the Fan Museum (tel: 020-8305 1441; Tue–Sat 11am–5pm Sun noon–5pm; charge). Its collection of 3,500 fans from around the world date from the 11th century to the present. Look out for the Fabergé *point de gaze* lace fan surrounded by rose diamonds. If you can afford it, you can even commission your own elaborate fan to be made by the museum.

gallery (with the tunic he was wearing when fatally wounded at Trafalgar – you can even see the musket-ball hole).

The Queen's House
Now walk along the colonnade to the **Queen's House** ❺ (opening times as for the National Maritime Museum, above). Construction on this, England's first Palladian villa, began in 1616, to designs by Inigo Jones. Intended for James I's Queen Anne, it was only completed after her death, and was then given by Charles I to Henrietta Maria. She stayed here only briefly, as in 1642 the Civil War broke out.

Today, the house is used to display the National Maritime Museum's art collection, with seascapes and portraits by, among others, Joshua Reynolds and Thomas Gainsborough. The real attraction, however, is the architecture,

which is sublime and deceptively simple: the Tulip Stairs, for example, were the first centrally unsupported spiral stairs constructed in England.

NAVAL COLLEGE

Next cross over the road and enter the **Old Royal Naval College** ❻ (tel: 020-8269 4747; daily: grounds 8am–6pm, hall and chapel 10am–5pm; free) by the Romney Road Gate. Built on the site of the Tudor royal palace of Placentia (birthplace of Elizabeth I), the complex was founded in 1694 as a hospital for elderly and infirm seamen. Sir Christopher Wren was appointed architect, and laid out all the foundations early on, so that future architects would have to fulfil his masterplan.

By the 19th century, British naval supremacy meant fewer casualties of war, and during the 1860s the hospital closed. In 1873 the Royal Naval College moved in; young officers were trained here until 1998, when the College passed to the Greenwich Foundation.

Today, only the 'Painted Hall' and the chapel are open to the public. The Painted Hall was originally intended as the dining room for the hospital. Unfortunately, Sir James Thornhill took so long to paint it (1707–26) and made it so elaborate (he was paid by the yard) that injured sailors never got to eat there, and it became a tourist attraction. In 1806, Admiral Lord Nelson's body lay in state here following his death at the Battle of Trafalgar; over three days, up to 30,000 people came to view the body.

Food and Drink 🍴
② BAR DU MUSÉE
17 Nelson Road; tel: 020-8858 4710; daily L and D; £££
An atmospheric bar at the front, and behind, a restaurant with garden for outside dining in summer. Bistro-style food. Service can be a little slow.

③ ADMIRAL HARDY
7 College Approach, Greenwich; tel: 020-8858 6452; daily L and D; ££
Comfortable pub built in 1830 and named after the admiral from whom Nelson received his dying kiss. Reasonable beer and food, including roast beef and Yorkshire pudding on Sundays. A haven for men whose wives or girlfriends are shopping in the covered market behind.

The chapel, completed in 1789, is an unaltered example of the Greek-revival style of James 'Athenian' Stuart, with its Classical columns and motifs. Worthy of contemplation inside is the altarpiece by the American painter, Benjamin West; it shows the story of St Paul's shipwreck on the Island of Malta.

COVERED MARKET

Leave the Naval College grounds by the west side on to King William Walk and cross the road to the **Covered Market** ❼ (www.greenwich-market. co.uk; Thur–Fri 7.30am–5.30pm, Sat, Sun 9.30am–5.30pm). Here, you can browse the food, jewellery, clothing, toiletries and gift stalls, and the shops alongside, or visit a pub or restaurant, see ⑪② and ⑪③, for refreshment.

GREENWICH PARK

From the Covered Market, return to King William Walk and head south, down the side of the Maritime Museum and through the gates into **Greenwich Park** (tel: 020-8858 2608; www.royal parks.org.uk; daily 6am–dusk; free).

Observatory and Planetarium

Follow the park's main road up the hill to the **Old Royal Observatory** ❽ (tel: 020-8312 8565; daily 10am–5pm; free). Founded by Charles II in 1675 to study astronomy and to fix longitude, it was designed by Wren (an amateur astronomer) for Flamsteed, the Astronomer Royal, who lived and worked here until his death in 1719. Today, scientific

instruments are exhibited, including sundials, atomic clocks, and Harrison's marine chronometers.

On the roof is a time ball, erected in 1833. At 12.55pm every day the ball rises up the pole, reaching the top at 12.58pm, and then dropping at exactly 1pm. The ball can be clearly seen from the river, and ships used to use it to check their time. In the courtyard below, brass strips set in the ground mark the **Greenwich Meridian**, the line dividing the eastern and western hemispheres.

Nearby is the South Building, housing the **Planetarium** (tel: 020-8312 8575; shows on the hour: Mon–Fri 1–4pm, Sat and Sun 11am–4pm; charge).

After admiring the view, wander back to the town, though if you have children, you may want to visit the boating pond (north-east of the Observatory) or the playground by the Maritime Museum.

Vanbrugh's House
On the eastern edge of the park is a fortress-like folly *(pictured above)*, built in 1719 by Sir John Vanbrugh, the architect and dramatist, for his own occupation while he was Surveyor to the Royal Naval Hospital. The castle is modelled on the French Bastille, where Vanbrugh was imprisoned on charges of spying for the British in 1690–2.

The Ranger's House

On the western edge of Greenwich Park, on Chesterfield Walk, is the Ranger's House (tel: 020-8853 0035; Apr–Sept: Mon–Wed and Sun 10am–5pm; charge). An elegant Georgian villa built in 1723, it became the official residence of the 'Ranger of Greenwich Park' after 1815, when the post was held by Princess Sophia Matilda, niece of George III. Today it houses the collection of the diamond magnate Sir Julius Wernher (1850–1912). Among the 700 works of art on display are early religious paintings, Dutch Old Masters, carved Gothic ivories, Renaissance bronzes and fine silver.

KEW

The south-western London suburb of Kew is synonymous with its royal bot-anic gardens, where, in 300 acres (120ha), are 30,000 types of plants, dozens of follies, plus glasshouses, lakes, ponds and even a Chinese pagoda. This route shows you some of its highlights and allows a leisurely ramble round the rest.

Steam Museum
Across the river from Kew Gardens is Kew Bridge Steam Museum (Green Dragon Lane; tel: 020-8568 4757; Tue–Sun 11am–5pm; charge, though children under 16 free). Inside a Victorian water works are steam pumping engines, while outside is a narrow gauge railway, which operates at weekends. To find the museum, follow Kew Road north, cross the bridge, turn left on to Kew Bridge Road and then right on to Green Dragon Lane.

DISTANCE 2 miles (3km)
TIME Half to a full day
START/END Kew Gardens tube
POINTS TO NOTE

The best way to get to Kew from central London is by tube: buy a ticket for zone 3 and take a westbound train on the Richmond branch of the District line. From the tube station, Kew Gardens are a few minutes' walk up Station Parade and then Lichfield Road. Alternatively, take a train from Waterloo to Kew Bridge.

Food and Drink

① **THE ORANGERY**
Kew Gardens; tel: 020-8332 5686; daily B, L and T, 10am until one hour before the gardens close; ££
Never successful as a hothouse for growing oranges (the light levels are too low), this classical building by Sir William Chambers is, however, a fine setting for a restaurant. On offer are salads, pasta, sandwiches and cakes.

② **MA CUISINE**
9 Station Approach; tel: 020-8332 1923; daily B, L and D; £££
The best-value restaurant in the area (note especially the lunchtime set menus). Recreates the classic French bistro experience, with homely cooking and rickety furniture.

In the leafy suburb of Kew are the **Royal Botanic Gardens** (tel: 020-8332 5655; www.kew.org.uk; summer: Mon–Fri 9.30am–6.30pm, Sat, Sun till 7.30pm, winter: 9.30am–4.15pm; glasshouses and museums close half an hour earlier than the gardens; charge, though free for children under 17 years). Passing into royal hands in the 1720s, the gardens were created by Prince Frederick, son of George II, in 1731. His widow, Augusta, introduced the botanical ele-ment in 1759, and the grounds were subsequently landscaped by that most renowned of all gardeners, 'Capability' Brown. Kew became famous, though, when the botanist Sir Joseph Banks returned in 1771 from his global travels with Captain Cook, bringing back many strange and exotic plants, and cultivating them in the royal gardens here.

PALM HOUSE AND LAKE

Enter the gardens by the **Victoria Gate ❶**, then pick up a map and head north towards the **Palm House ❷**, which fronts on to a lake. Designed by Decimus Burton, the Palm House was completed in 1848 and was the first large-scale wrought-iron structure of its kind. Each of its iridescent panes of glass is hand-blown. Inside, climb

up the spiral stairs through the steamy tropical atmosphere to the galleries and inspect the canopy of banana trees, coconuts and pawpaws.

In the basement is the **Marine Display**, with tanks of corals, fish, algae and mangrove swamps. Just to the side of the Palm House is the **Waterlily House ❸**, encompassing a circular pond covered in giant Amazonian waterlilies.

Outside, on the opposite side of the lake, is another Decimus Burton creation, the **Plants and People Museum ❹**, illustrating mankind's dependence on plants, with exhibits displayed in the museum's fine original Victorian mahogany cabinets.

PRINCESS OF WALES CONSERVATORY

Continuing north-east beyond the lake, follow the signs for the **Princess of Wales Conservatory ❺**. This glasshouse is divided into 10 micro-climates, suitable for everything from cacti to carnivorous plants. It is particularly worth seeking out the *titan arum* − equally renowned for being the world's largest flower, for its foul smell (like rotting flesh) and for its rare flowerings.

KEW PALACE

Next, heading north-west, take some refreshment at the **Orangery**, see ⓦ①, en route to **Kew Palace ❻** (Apr–Sept: daily 10am–5pm; charge). Originally built for a Dutch merchant, Britain's smallest palace was leased to Queen Caroline in 1728 for 'the rent of £100 and a fat Doe'. George III later bought the palace and recuperated here in his first period of madness. The garden behind is laid out in 17th-century style with parterres of box and varieties of herbs, and statuary, as ornamentation.

If your time is up, retrace your steps back to the tube. For those looking for a restaurant before the journey back to central London, consider **Ma Cuisine**, see ⓦ②, just off Station Parade.

Above from far left: Palm House; Temperate House; *Pink Rhododendron* by Sally Keir, in the Shirley Sherwood Gallery; Waterlily House. **Below left:** Kew Palace.

Hampton Court
In the summer, it is possible to visit Kew Gardens in the morning and Hampton Court in the afternoon. Boats leave from Kew at 1.30pm for Hampton Court and return again at 3pm, 4pm and 5pm. For more information and to check times, call Westminster Piers on 020-7930 4721.

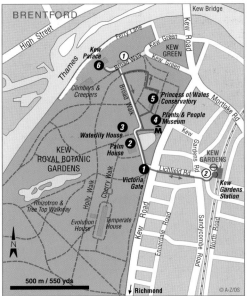

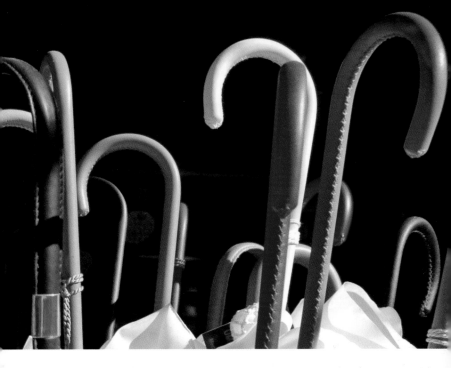

DIRECTORY

A user-friendly alphabetical listing of practical information, plus hand-picked hotels and restaurants, clearly organised by area, to suit all budgets and tastes.

A–Z   102

ACCOMMODATION   112

RESTAURANTS   118

A

AIRPORTS AND ARRIVAL

(See also Public Transport)
Airports

London has two major international airports: Heathrow, 15 miles (24km) to the west (mainly scheduled flights) and Gatwick, 25 miles (40km) to the south (scheduled and charter flights), plus three smaller airports, Stansted and Luton to the north and London City to the east.

Heathrow: The fastest connection to central London is the Heathrow Express to Paddington station, which runs every 15 minutes between around 5am and 11.45pm, taking 15 minutes. Paddington then connects with several tube lines *(see map inside back cover)*. The fare is £14.50 single, or £28 return (tel: 0845-600 1515). A cheaper option is the 25-minute Heathrow Connect service, which stops at several stations; a single costs £6.90 (tel: 08457 484 950).

There is a direct tube route (£4 single) on the Piccadilly line, which reaches central London in about 50 minutes, via Kensington, Knightsbridge and Piccadilly to King's Cross, and operates daily from 5am (6am on Sun) until 11.40pm.

National Express runs coaches from Heathrow's central bus station to Victoria Coach Station; journey time 45–80 minutes, depending on traffic; single £10. For information, tel: 0870-580 8080, www.nationalexpress.com.

Gatwick: The Gatwick Express train leaves Gatwick for Victoria Station every 15 minutes, 4.35am–1.35am. It takes 30 minutes and costs £14.90 one-way. You can also take non-express services to Victoria and King's Cross. A single to either costs £8.90 and takes 35–45 minutes.

Stansted: The Stansted Express direct rail link goes to Liverpool Street Station every 15 minutes; journey time is 45 minutes; a single costs £14.50.

London City: The DLR stop for London City Airport is six minutes from Canning Town tube (Jubilee line), running every 10 minutes from 5.30am–1.15am.

Luton: Luton Airport Parkway rail is linked by Thameslink services to King's Cross and Blackfriars, taking 40 minutes and running around every 15 minutes on weekdays only.

Arrival By Train

Eurostar services from Paris Gare du Nord take around 2¼ hours (Paris, tel: 0033 8 92 35 35 39), and from Brussels 2 hours (Brussels, tel: 0032 25 28 28 28) to the terminal at London St Pancras. For UK bookings, tel: 0870-518 6186. Also visit www.eurostar.com.

Vehicles are also carried by **Le Shuttle** trains through the tunnel between Folkestone in Kent and Sangatte in France. There are two to five departures each hour, and the trip takes 35 minutes. Bookings are not essential, but advisable at peak times. Fares vary according to

Airport Numbers
Heathrow,
tel: 0870-000 0123
Gatwick,
tel: 0870-000 2468
Luton,
tel: 01582-405100
Stansted,
tel: 0870-000 0303
London City,
tel: 020-7646 0000

the time of travel and how far in advance you book: late at night or early morning are usually cheaper. Taking a car (with any number of passengers) through the tunnel costs from about £122 return, or €188. For information and reservations, tel: 08705 353535 (UK), 0810 63 03 04 (France), or visit www.eurotunnel.com.

C

CHILDREN

Public Transport: Up to four children aged 11 or under can travel free on the tube if accompanied by an adult with a ticket. Unlimited off-peak travel is available to 11- to 13-year-olds for £1 per day or 'Kids for a Quid' single fares if travelling with an Oyster- or Travelcard-holding adult; likewise 14- to 15-year-olds who have a photo Oyster card (which can take up to two weeks to obtain). Buses are free for all children under 16, but 14- to 15-year-olds need a 14–15 Oyster photocard.

Supplies: Infant formula and nappies (diapers) can be found in chemists (pharmacies) and supermarkets. If you require over-the-counter medications such as Calpol (liquid paracetamol) late at night, Bliss Pharmacy (5 Marble Arch; tel: 020-7723 6116) is open daily until midnight.

CLIMATE

London's climate is generally mild all year round. Snow is unusual, and January temperatures average 6°C (43°F).

Temperatures in the summer months average 18°C (64°F), but they can soar, causing the city to become very stuffy (air conditioning is not universal). It often rains, so keep an umbrella handy at all times.

CRIME

Hold on to your handbag (purse) and keep your wallet in a breast pocket in public. Be on your guard after dark away from crowded streets and in the Underground. Use only licensed minicabs and black cabs.

In an emergency, dial 999 from any telephone (no money or card necessary). Otherwise telephone the nearest police station, listed under 'Police' in the telephone directory.

CUSTOMS REGULATIONS

There are no official restrictions on the movement of goods within the European Union (EU), provided those goods were purchased within the EU. However, British Customs have set the following personal-use 'guide levels':

Tobacco: 3,200 cigarettes or 400 cigarillos or 200 cigars or 3kg tobacco. (Limits are 200 cigarettes or 250g of smoking tobacco if coming from Bulgaria, Czech Republic, Estonia, Hungary, Latvia, Lithuania, Poland, Romania, Slovakia and Slovenia.)

Alcohol: 10 litres spirits, 20 litres fortified wines, 90 litres wine, 110 litres beer.

Those entering from a non-EU state are subject to these limits:

Above from far left: children at the Natural History Museum; desirable London address.

Tobacco: 200 cigarettes or 100 cigarillos or 50 cigars or 250g of tobacco.

Alcohol: 1 litre of spirits, or 2 litres of fortified or sparkling wine, or 2 litres of table wine (an additional 2 litres of still wine if no spirits are bought).

Perfume: 60cc perfume and 250cc toilet water.

There are no restrictions on the amount of currency you can bring in.

CYCLING

Route maps specifically aimed at cyclists are available from the London Cycling Campaign (www.lcc.org.uk) or London Cycle Network (www.london cycle network.org.uk). Note that great care is necessary when cycling in London, as traffic is usually heavy.

D

DISABLED ACCESS

An excellent guidebook is *Access in London* by Gordon Couch, William Forrester and Justin Irwin (Quiller Press). The London Tourist Board also provides a free leaflet, *London For All*, available from Information Centres. For details on public transport pick up *Access to the Underground* (free from ticket offices) and Transport for London's *Access to Mobility* (www.tfl.gov.uk).

Artsline is a free telephone information service for disabled people in London, covering the arts and entertainment (tel: 020-7388 2227; www. artsline.org.uk), Mon–Fri 9.30am–5.30pm.

Cycle Hire
Reputable bike-hire firms in London include: Banana Rent (tel: 0845 644 2868; www. bananarent.com); London Bicycle Tour Company (tel: 020-7928 6838; www.londonbicycle. com); and OY Bike (tel: 0845 226 5571; www. oybike.com).

DRIVING

Unless you are planning on making several trips outside the capital, a car is most likely to be more of a hindrance than a help, and certainly a considerable expense, owing to the congestion charge *(see below)* and the high cost of parking. Negotiating Central London in a car is stressful, owing to the city's impatient drivers and web of one-way streets.

If you must hire a car, remember to drive on the left and observe the speed limits (police detection cameras are increasingly common). It is strictly illegal to drink and drive, and penalties are severe. The law also states that drivers and passengers must wear seat belts. For further information on driving in Britain consult the *Highway Code*.

Congestion Charge: Cars driving into a clearly marked Congestion Zone, extending between Kensington and the City, between 7am and 6.30pm Mon–Fri are filmed, and their drivers are fined if a payment of £8 has not been made by midnight the same day (or £10 the following day). You can pay at many small shops, including newsagents, by phone (tel: 0845 900 1234) or at www.cclondon.com.

Fuel: Petrol (gasoline) is sold at filling stations and outside many supermarkets (priced in litres).

Parking: This is a big problem in congested central London. Meters are slightly less expensive than NCP (multi-

storey) car parks, but some only allow parking for a maximum of two hours; it can also be hard to find a free one. Do not leave your car parked on a meter a moment longer than your time allows and do not return and insert more money once your time has run out – both are finable offences. Most meter parking is free after 6.30pm daily and after 1.30pm in most areas on Saturday and all day Sunday, but always check this on the meter.

Speed Limits: Unless otherwise indicated these are: 30mph (50kph) in urban areas, 60mph (100kph) on normal roads away from built-up areas, 70mph (112kph) on motorways and dual carriageways.

Breakdown. The following organisations operate 24-hour breakdown assistance to their members: AA, tel: 0800 887 766; RAC, tel: 0800 828 282.

ELECTRICITY

The standard current in Britain is 240 volt, 50 cycle AC. Plugs have three pins rather than two, so bring an adaptor if necessary.

EMBASSIES

Australia: Australia House, Strand, WC2B 4LA; tel: 020-7379 4334
Canada: Macdonald House, 1 Grosvenor Square, W1X 4AB; tel: 020-7258 6600

Ireland: 17 Grosvenor Place, SW1X 7HR; tel: 020-7235 2171
New Zealand: 80 Haymarket, SW1Y 4TQ; tel: 020-7930 8422
US: 24 Grosvenor Square, W1A 1AE; tel: 020-7499 9000

EMERGENCIES

For police, fire brigade or ambulance dial **999** from any telephone (no money or card required) and tell the operator which service you require.

ENTRY REQUIREMENTS

To enter Britain you need a valid passport (or any form of official identification if you are an EU citizen). Visas are not needed if you are from the US, a Commonwealth citizen or an EU national (or from most other European or South American countries). Health certificates are not required unless you have arrived from Asia, Africa or South America. If you wish to stay for a protracted period or apply to work, contact the Border and Immigration Agency. First look at the website www.ind.homeoffice.gov.uk. London's nearest Public Enquiry Office (PEO) is Lunar House, 40 Wellesley Road, Croydon, CR9 2BY; tel: 0870-606 7766.

FURTHER READING

A Literary Guide to London by Ed Glinet. Detailed street-by-street guide.

Above from far left: Congestion Charge sign; traffic wardens having a field day.

London: The Biography by Peter Ackroyd. Readable anecdotal history.

London Orbital by Iain Sinclair. A walk round the M25; surprisingly engrossing.

London Under London by Richard Trench and Ellis Hillman. Traces the maze of tunnels beneath the streets.

Oliver Twist or *Bleak House* by Charles Dickens. Classic London novels.

Soho in the Fifties by Daniel Farson. Portrait of Soho in its louche heyday.

G

GAY AND LESBIAN

With Europe's largest gay and lesbian population, London has an abundance of bars, restaurants and clubs to cater for most tastes, with the scene focusing around Soho, Earl's Court and Vauxhall. For listings, consult the free gay weekly magazines, *Boyz*, the *Pink Paper* and *QX*. Monthly magazines for sale include *Gay Times*, *Diva* and *Attitude*.

Useful telephone contacts for advice and counselling include London Lesbian and Gay Switchboard (tel: 020-7837 7324) and London Friend (7.30–10pm; tel: 020-7837 3337).

H

HEALTH AND MEDICAL CARE

EU citizens can receive free treatment on producing a European Health Insurance Card. Citizens of other countries must pay, except for emergency treatment (always free). Major hospitals include Charing Cross Hospital (Fulham Palace Road, W6, tel: 020-8846 1234) and St Thomas's (Lambeth Palace Road, SE1, tel: 020-7188 7188). Guy's Hospital Dental Department is at St Thomas Street, SE1, tel: 020-7188 0512. For the nearest hospital or doctor's, ring NHS Direct, tel: 0845 46 47. Late pharmacy: Bliss Chemist, 5 Marble Arch, W1, opens till midnight.

I

INTERNET

Free wi-fi internet access is becoming increasingly common in London, in coffee shops, hotels, pubs and bookstores. Pay-as-you-go internet access is available at many venues including the easy chain, www.easyeverything.com.

L

LEFT LUGGAGE

Most of the capital's main railway stations have left-luggage departments where you can leave your suitcases on a short-term basis, although all are extremely sensitive to potential terrorist bombs. Left-luggage offices close at around 10pm (including St Pancras) or 11pm with the exception of Victoria, which remains open until midnight.

LOST PROPERTY

For possessions lost on public transport or in taxis, contact Transport for London's central Lost Property, 200 Baker

Street, NW1 5RZ (tel: 0845 330 9882) Mon–Fri 8.30am–4pm, or fill in an enquiry form, available from any London Underground station or bus garage.

If you lose your passport, let your embassy know as well as the nearest police station (for numbers of these, call directory enquiries on 118 500, 118 888 or 118 811).

MAPS

For detailed exploration of the city centre and suburbs, the London *A–Z* books, with all roads indexed, come in various formats. Free tube maps are available at Underground stations.

MEDIA

Newspapers: Daily national papers include the *Daily Telegraph* and *The Times* (both on the right politically), *The Independent* (in the middle) and *The Guardian* (left of centre). Most have Sunday equivalents. The *Financial Times* is more business and finance orientated. Except for the *Daily Mirror*, the tabloids (*The Sun, Star, Daily Mail, Daily Express* and *Metro*) are right-wing. The *Evening Standard* (Mon–Fri) is good for cinema and theatre listings. Foreign papers are sold at many news-stands and main railway stations.

There are several free papers produced specifically for commuters: *Metro*, in the mornings, and *The London Paper* and *London Lite*, in the evenings. All have useful listings sections.

Listings Magazines: Most comprehensive is the weekly *Time Out*.

Television: The BBC is financed by annual TV licences; ITV, Channel 4 (C4) and Five are funded by advertising. There are also scores of cable and satellite channels.

Radio: BBC stations include Radio 1 (98.8FM, pop), Radio 2 (89.2FM, easy listening), Radio 3 (91.3FM, classical music), Radio 4 (93.5FM, current affairs, plays, cultural discussions, etc), BBC London (94.9FM, music, chat) and BBC World Service (648 kHz, news). Commercial stations include Capital FM (96.8FM, pop), Jazz FM (102.2FM) and Classic FM (100.9FM).

MONEY

Currency: The monetary unit is the pound sterling (£), divided into 100 pence (p). Bank notes: £5, £10, £20, £50. Coins: 1p, 2p, 5p, 10p, 20p, 50p, £1, £2. Some of London's large stores also accept euros.

Banks: These usually open 9.30am– 4.30/5pm Monday to Friday, with Saturday morning banking common in shopping areas. Major English banks tend to offer similar exchange rates, so it is only worth looking around if you have large amounts of money to change. Banks charge no commission on sterling travellers' cheques, and if a London bank is affiliated to your own bank, it will not charge for cheques in other currencies either.

However, there will be a charge for changing cash into another currency. You will need ID such as a passport in order to change travellers' cheques.

ATMs. The easiest way to take out currency is using an ATM, known as a cashpoint or cash machine, using your everyday bank card. The best rates are also usually available this way. There are myriad cash machines across London, inside and outside banks, in supermarkets and at rail and tube stations. They operate on global credit and debit systems including Maestro/Cirrus, Switch, Visa and others. ATMs are accessed using a PIN code comprised of numbers.

Credit Cards: International credit cards are almost universally accepted in shops, restaurants, hotels etc. Signs on display at the entrance or next to the till should confirm which cards are accepted.

Currency Exchange: Some high-street travel agents, such as Thomas Cook, operate bureaux de change at comparable rates. There are also private bureaux de change (some are open 24 hours), where rates are sometimes very low and commissions high. If you do use one, ensure it carries a London Tourist Board code of conduct sticker.

P

POSTAL SERVICES

Most post offices open Mon–Fri 9am–5pm, Sat 9am–noon. Stamps are available from post offices and selected shops, usually newsagents, and from machines outside some post offices. There is a two-tier service within the UK: first class is supposed to reach a UK destination the next day, second class will take at least a day or two longer. London's main post office (24–8 William IV Street; Mon, Wed–Fri 8.30am–6.30pm, Tue open from 9.15am, Sat 9am–5.30pm) is by Trafalgar Square, behind the church of St Martin-in-the-Fields.

The cost of sending a letter or parcel depends on weight and size.

POSTCODES

The first half of London postcodes indicate the general area (WC = West Central, SE = South East) and the second half, used only for mail, identifies the exact block. Here is a key to some of the commoner codes:

W1 Mayfair, Marylebone, Soho; W2 Bayswater; W4 Chiswick; W8 Kensington; W11 Notting Hill; WC1 Bloomsbury; WC2 Covent Garden, Strand; E1 Whitechapel; EC1 Clerkenwell; EC2 Bank, Barbican; EC4 St Paul's, Blackfriars; SW1 St James's, Belgravia; SW3 Chelsea; SW7 Knightsbridge, South Kensington; SW19 Wimbledon; SE1 Lambeth, Southwark; SE10 Greenwich; SE21 Dulwich; N1 Hoxton, Islington; N6 Highgate; NW3 Hampstead.

PUBLIC HOLIDAYS

1 Jan: New Year's Day
Mar/Apr: Good Fri; Easter Mon

May: May Day (first Mon of month); Spring Bank Holiday (last Mon)
Aug: Summer Bank Holiday (last Mon of month)
25 Dec: Christmas Day
26 Dec: Boxing Day

PUBLIC TRANSPORT

London's transport map is divided into six zones, spreading outwards from central London (zone 1) to cover all of Greater London. Tube and rail fares are priced according to which zones you travel in. Day travelcards enable unlimited tube, DLR, rail and bus travel in specified zones and start at £5.10 for Zones 1–2, off-peak (after 9.30am).

Underground (tube)

The fastest and easiest way to get around London is by tube. Try to avoid the rush hours (8am–9.30am and 5–6.30pm), when trains are packed with commuters. Services run from 5.30am to just after midnight. Make sure you have a ticket and keep hold of it after you have passed through the barrier; you will need it to exit.

There is a flat rate of £4 for a single tube journey across any zones. Oyster Cards *(see box, right)* are a wise buy if you plan to travel a lot by tube. For enquiries, tel: 020-7222 1234; www.tfl.gov.uk.

Docklands Light Railway

The DLR runs from Bank and Tower Gateway to east and south-east London destinations. Tickets are the same type and cost as for the tube.

Rail

London's commuter rail network provides links to areas not on underground lines; travelcards are still valid on rail services for journeys within the correct zones. Thameslink services run through the city centre, while the London Overground connects Richmond with Stratford via the north of the capital. Other services run out of London's major rail stations, including Waterloo, King's Cross, London Bridge and Liverpool Street. For times and enquiries tel: 08457 484 950; www.nationalrail.co.uk.

Bus

If you are not in a hurry, travel by bus provides a good way of seeing London;

Above from far left: buses always come in multiples; Gatwick Express.

Tube Marathon
There are 275 stations on the Underground network, and the fastest time taken to visit every one currently stands at 19 hours.

Tickets and Fares

Single tickets on London's transport networks are very expensive, so it's best to buy one of several multi-journey passes. London is divided into six fare zones, with zones 1–2 covering all of central London. Travelcards give unlimited travel on the tube, buses and DLR. A one-day Travelcard for zones 1 and 2 and off-peak (valid after 9.30am) costs £5.10 (£3.30, children aged 5–15). You can also buy three-day or seven-day cards. Oystercards are smart cards that you charge up with credit (using cash or a credit card), then touch in on card readers at tube stations and on buses, so that an amount is deducted each time you use it. They are cheaper than Travelcards if you only expect to travel a few times each day. Cards and Oysters can be bought from tube and DLR stations and newsagents. Visitors can order them ahead from www.visitbritaindirect.com. Children under 16 travel for free at all times on buses, and under-11s travel free on the tube and DLR at off-peak times provided they are with an adult. For full details of all fares, see www.tfl.gov.uk.

LONDON

the bus network is very comprehensive. The flat fare is £2. Again, an Oyster Card is the best bet, as each journey then costs £1, and the total is price-capped at £3 per day. You can get a one-day pass for £3.50 or a seven-day pass for £14. Night buses run all night on the most popular routes. Full bus route maps are available at Travel Information Centres.

Boat

River cruises are a great way to see London's sights and various routes run on the Thames between Hampton Court and Barrier Gardens. There is a hop-on-hop-off River Rover pass (£11 per adult); see www.citycruises.com.

SMOKING

Since July 2007 smoking in all enclosed public spaces, including pubs, clubs and bars (though not in outside beer gardens) has been banned in England.

STUDENT TRAVELLERS

International students can obtain various discounts at attractions, on travel services (including Eurostar) and in some shops by showing a valid ISIC card; see www.isiccard.com for details.

T

TAXIS

Black cabs are licensed and display the charges on the meter. They can be hailed in the street if their 'for hire' sign is lit. There are also ranks at major train stations and at various points across the city, or you can order a cab on 0871 871 8710. All black cabs are wheelchair accessible.

Minicabs should only be hired by phone; they are not allowed to pick up passengers on the street. Reputable firms include: Addison Lee, tel: 020-7387 8888; www.addisonlee.com.

TELEPHONES

London's UK dialling code is 020. To call from abroad, dial '44', the international access code for Britain, then 20 (the London code, with the initial '0' dropped), then the eight-digit individual number.

To phone abroad, dial 00 followed by the international code for the country you want, then the number: Australia (61); Ireland (353); US and Canada (1), etc. If using a US credit phone card, first dial the company's access number as follows: Sprint, tel: 0800 890 877; MCI, tel: 0800 890 222; AT&T, tel: 0800 890 011.

Despite the ubiquity of mobiles (cellphones), London still has a fair number of public phone boxes; most accept phone cards, which are widely available from post offices and newsagents in amounts from £1 to £20. At coin phone boxes, the smallest coin accepted is 20p.

Useful Numbers

Emergency – police, fire, ambulance: tel: 999

Operator (for difficulties in getting through): tel: 100
International Operator: tel: 155
Directory Enquiries (UK): tel: 118500 or 118888 or 118811
International Directory Enquiries: tel: 118 505 or 118 866 or 118 899

TIME

In winter, Great Britain is on Greenwich Mean Time, which is 8 hours ahead of Los Angeles, 5 hours in front of New York and Montreal, and 10 hours behind Sydney. During the summer, from the last Sunday in March to the last Sunday in October, clocks are put forward one hour.

TOUR OPERATORS

The **Original Tour** (tel: 020-8877 2120; www.theoriginaltour.com) is the biggest London sightseeing operator, and operates all year round. You hop on and hop off at over 90 different stops and enjoy a commentary in a wide choice of languages. There is also a Kids' Club for 5- to 12-year-olds. Purchase tickets on the bus or in advance.

Big Bus Company (tel: 020-7233 9533; www.bigbustours.com) operates three routes of hop-on hop-off services.

Duck Tours (tel: 020-7928 3132; www. londonducktours.co.uk) employ World War II amphibious vehicles, which leave from County Hall, then drive past famous London landmarks before taking to the water on the Thames. Good fun for children.

TOURIST OFFICES

The offical tourist board (www.visit london.com) offers information on sights, events and practical points, plus a commercial hotel booking service.

Personal enquiries can be made at Britain and London Visitor Centre, 1 Regent Street, Piccadilly Circus, SW1Y 4XT (Mon 9.30am–6.30pm, Tue–Fri 9am–6.30pm, Sat and Sun 10am–4pm, except Jun–Sept: Sat 9am–5pm).

There are other tourist information in the City (St Paul's Churchyard; tel: 020-7332 1456); Greenwich (Pepys House, 2 Cutty Sark Gardens; tel: 0870 608 2000) and on the South Bank (Vinopolis, 1 Bank End; tel: 020 7357 9168).

W
WEBSITES

In addition to the many websites listed in this guidebook, the following are useful for information on London: www.bbc.co.uk/london (BBC London) www.thisislondon.com (*Evening Standard* site; useful listings) www.metro.co.uk (*Metro* newspaper) www.london-se1.co.uk (information on the South Bank and Bankside) www.streetmap.co.uk (address locator) www.24hourmuseum.co.uk (up-to-date information on museum shows)

WEIGHTS AND MEASURES

Although distances are still measured in miles, and drinks are served as pints, all goods must officially be sold in metric.

Above from far left: Port Authority sign near Smithfield Market; taxi queue at Victoria Station.

Toilets
Public conveniences can usually be found in railway stations, parks and museums. Underground stations do not normally have toilets. There is often, although not always, a charge of 10p or 20p to use public toilets, and you may find that those in pubs or bars are reserved for customer use only. The majority of large department stores have free customer toilets.

Soho and Covent Garden

Covent Garden Hotel

10 Monmouth Street, WC2; tel: 020-7806 1000; www.firmdale.com; tube: Covent Garden; £££

Understatedly chic boutique hotel, popular with visiting film stars. As well as its 58 rooms styled with a contemporary English aesthetic, the hotel also offers a luxurious film screening room, a DVD library, a gym and a beauty salon.

Hazlitt's

6 Frith Street, W1; tel: 020-7434 1771; www.hazlittshotel.com; tube: Tottenham Court Road; ££

In the heart of Soho, this gorgeous converted 1718 house has several impressive literary connections *(see p.38)*. Rooms are in period style, and modern luxuries subtly tucked away.

One Aldwych

1 Aldwych, WC2; tel: 020-7300 1000; www.onealdwych.co.uk; tube: Temple, Covent Garden; ££££

Trying a little too hard to be stylish, with its corporate artworks and swimming pool with underwater music, this hotel does nevertheless offer good service in a great location.

Royal Adelphi Hotel

21 Villiers Street, WC2; tel: 020-7930 8764; www.royaladelphi.co.uk; tube: Charing Cross; £

This B&B is extremely good value for its central, bustling location, a couple of minutes' walk from Trafalgar Square. Basic but clean, with large bathrooms.

St Martin's Lane

45 St Martin's Lane, WC2; tel: 020-7300 5500; www.stmartinslane.com; tube: Leicester Square; ££££

This Starck/Schrager collaboration is one of the most stylish and stylised hotels in town. The rooms have high windows and mood-lighting options. Well placed for West End theatres.

Sanderson Hotel

50 Berners Street, W1; tel: 020-7300 9500; www.sandersonlondon.com; tube: Oxford Circus; ££££

Another Starck/Schrager creation, and the acme of their modernism-meets-theatre ethos. The Long Bar and Spoon restaurant are destinations in themselves, and the spa is fittingly opulent.

The Savoy

Strand, WC2; tel: 020-7836 4343; www.fairmont.com/savoy; tube: Charing Cross; £££

One of London's top hotels. Reopens in 2009 after £100-million refurbishment.

Soho Hotel

4 Richmond Mews, W1; tel: 020-7559 3000; www.firmdale.com; tube: Tottenham Court Road; £££

With bold, modern design touches in Kit Kemp's signature style, this hotel feels luxuriously urban, with dramatic drawing rooms and a buzzing bar.

Mayfair and Piccadilly

Brown's Hotel

30 Albemarle Street, W1; tel: 020-7493 6020; www.brownshotel.com; tube: Green Park; ££££

Opened in 1837 by Lord Byron's butler, James Brown, this classic luxury Mayfair hotel is now owned by Rocco Forte and has just been revamped to give it a contemporary, elegant look.

Claridge's

Brook Street, W1, tel: 020-7629 8860; www.savoygroup.com; tube: Bond Street; ££££

For many, the embodiment of English hotel graciousness, Claridge's was popular with exiled European royalty in World War II. The rooms are elegant late Victorian or Art Deco in style, and top chef Gordon Ramsay heads the restaurant.

Cumberland Hotel

Great Cumberland Place, W1; tel: 0870 400 8701; www.guoman. com; tube: Marble Arch; ££

Sleek minimalist decor both in the public rooms and the hi-tech guest rooms. Celebrity chef Gary Rhodes runs the restaurant. Good business facilities.

The Dorchester

Park Lane, W1; tel: 020-7629 8888; www.dorchesterhotel.com; tube: Hyde Park Corner; ££££

Large luxury hotel. Rooms have traditional decor and some have views over Hyde Park. The spa and the prestige restaurants (including China Tang and Alain Ducasse) are the main draw.

Duke's Hotel

35 St James's Place, SW1; tel: 020-7491 4840; www.dukeshotel.com; tube: Green Park; £££

Traditional hotel with gas-lamps lighting the courtyard, and an intimate atmosphere. The comfortable rooms are decorated in a classic, understated style. Quality without ostentation.

Durrants Hotel

George Street, W1; tel: 020-7935 8131; www.durrantshotel.co.uk; tube: Marble Arch; ££

A traditional family-run hotel in a Georgian terrace. Rooms are comfortable, with some antique furnishings.

Edward Lear Hotel

30 Seymour Street, W1; tel: 020-7402 5401; www.edlear.com; tube: Marble Arch; £

Friendly hotel in the former home of the Victorian artist and nonsense poet, near Oxford Street. Simple furnishings, but great value in a good location.

Metropolitan

19 Old Park Lane, W1; tel: 020-7447 1000; www.metropolitan.co.uk; tube: Green Park; ££££

Synonymous with late-1990s celebrity hedonism, the bar is the most noted feature of this modern hotel. The rooms, however, are also worthy of mention, graced as they are with clean simple decor and abundant natural light.

Price for a double room for one night without breakfast:	
££££	over £300
£££	£200–300
££	£120–200
£	below £120

Above from far left: the Kipling Suite *(far left)* and swish hotel chair *(far right)* at Brown's Hotel; Soho Hotel; lobby at Duke's Hotel.

Airport Cabins

If you need to bed down at the airport prior to an early morning flight, consider Yotel (tel: 020-7100 1100; www.yotel.com) at Heathrow's Terminal 4 or Gatwick's South Terminal. Here, check into a luxurious cabin (as if in first class on an aircraft) for a few hours' kip at any time of day or night. Depending on demand, a double cabin costs about £80 a night, and a single about £55. Prices come down if you stay for less time (minimum 4 hours, from £25). Cabins have en-suite bathrooms, a TV-film system and free internet access.

Montcalm Hotel

34–40 Great Cumberland Place, W1; tel: 020-7402 4288; www.montcalm.co.uk; tube: Marble Arch; ££

Quiet, comfortable mid-range hotel in an elegant Georgian crescent. Features low-allergen bedrooms.

No. 5 Maddox Street

5 Maddox Street, W1; tel: 020-7647 0200; www.living-rooms.co.uk; tube: Bond Street; £££

Offers suites-cum-flats with minimalist, Eastern-inspired decor and full facilities including your own kitchen (stocked with health food as well as more wicked treats).

Pavilion

34–6 Sussex Gardens, W2; tel: 020-7262 0905; www.pavilionhoteluk.com; tube: Edgware Road; £

Eccentric hotel in which each of the rooms has a different theme, from 'Casablanca Nights', a Moorish fantasy, to the Orientally inspired 'Enter the Dragon'. Good-value fun.

Piccadilly Backpackers

12 Sherwood Street, W1; tel: 020-7434 9009; www.piccadillybackpackers.com; tube: Piccadilly Circus; £

Price for a double room for one night without breakfast:

££££	over £300
£££	£200–300
££	£120–200
£	below £120

If you are on a tight budget, and more interested in dancing than sleeping the night away, this Soho hostel is ideal. Dorm beds start at £12, and there are also 'pod'-style beds and private rooms.

The Ritz

150 Piccadilly, W1; tel: 020-7493 8181; www.theritzlondon.com; tube: Green Park; ££££

The lustre on the gilded interior has long since faded, and this now slightly shabby hotel relies more than anything on its famous name to draw people in for its highly priced afternoon teas. Men must wear jackets and ties in the public rooms, and no jeans or trainers allowed!

Sherlock Holmes Hotel

108 Baker Street, W1; tel: 020-7486 6161; www.sherlockholmeshotel.com; tube: Baker Street; ££

Ignore the connotations of the name: this is a boutique hotel with modern guest rooms, a gym and a steam room.

Westminster and Victoria

B&B Belgravia

64–6 Ebury Street, SW1; tel: 020-7823 4928; www.bb-belgravia.com; tube: Victoria; £

Chic, modern B&B offering good value for the style and facilities. These include: free DVD and internet use, a choice of organic breakfasts, and free bicycle hire.

Goring Hotel

15 Beeston Place, Grosvenor Gardens, SW1; tel: 020-7396 9000; www.goringhotel.co.uk; tube: Victoria; ££££

Traditional, family-owned, hotel close to Buckingham Palace. Elegant old-world interiors and service.

New England Hotel

20 St George's Drive, SW1; tel: 020-7834 8351; www.newenglandhotel.com; tube: Victoria; £

Friendly B&B in an elegant 19th-century stuccoed building in Pimlico.

Sanctuary House Hotel

33 Tothill Street, SW1; tel: 020-7799 4044; www.fullershotels.co.uk; tube: St James's Park; ££

Small, recently refurbished hotel above a Fullers Ale and Pie House.

Windermere Hotel

142–4 Warwick Way, SW1; tel: 020-7834 5163; www.windermere-hotel.co.uk; tube: Victoria; £

Well-run B&B with good-sized rooms in a typical Pimlico stuccoed hosue.

Kensington and Chelsea

Base2Stay

25 Courtfield Gardens, SW5; tel: 0845-262 8000; www.base2stay.com; tube: Earl's Court; £

Taking the principles and style of boutique hotels to the budget market, this hotel innovator offers 'studios', with their own fridges, microwaves and media facilities, to provide the freedom of a flat with the ease of a hotel.

Beaufort Hotel

33 Beaufort Gardens, SW3; tel: 020-7584 5252; www.thebeaufort.co.uk; tube: Knightsbridge; £££

Soft, neutral colours are indicative of the calm that prevails at this small, designer hotel. Attentive service. Cream teas and residents' bar included in the room rate.

Berkeley Hotel

Wilton Place, SW1; tel: 020-7235 6000; www.the-savoy-group.com; tube: Knightsbridge; ££££

Many rate the Berkeley as the best in London. Elegantly low-key, it offers a country-house atmosphere, a fine spa and rooftop pool, and restaurants run by Marcus Wareing and Gordon Ramsay.

Blakes Hotel

33 Roland Gardens, SW7; tel: 020-7370 6701; www.blakeshotel.com; tube: South Kensington; ££££

Anouska Hempel's original design hotel. The discreet exterior belies the splendid rooms, designed variously in romantic, grand and exotic styles.

Cadogan Hotel

75 Sloane Street, SW1; tel: 020-7235 7141; www.cadogan.com; tube: Sloane Square; ££££

An Edwardian-styled hotel with a whiff of scandal permeating its traditional formality. Edward VII's mistress Lillie Langtry lived at the Cadogan, and Oscar Wilde was arrested here.

Capital Hotel

22 Basil Street, SW3; tel: 020-7589 5171; www.capitalhotel.co.uk; tube: Knightsbridge; ££££

This small luxury hotel in the heart of Knightsbridge offers restrained decor, friendly service and a fine restaurant.

Above from far left: The Halkin; guest room *(centre left)* and decor to impress *(centre right)* at the Cadogan; Blakes.

Pampering
The Berkeley Hotel offers a 'Fashionista's Afternoon Tea' with champagne, cakes and pastries inspired by the season's catwalk designs, as well as, if you are interested, tea. Also on offer is a 'Girls Night In' (£425 for two people). It includes manicures, cocktails, goodie bag, ice cream, toiletries, smelly candles, CDs, DVDs and access to the spa and rooftop pool. What will they think of next?

The Gore

189 Queen's Gate, SW7; tel: 020-7584 6601; www.gorehotel.co.uk; tube: South Kensington; £££;

Idiosyncratic hotel close to the Royal Albert Hall. Every inch of the walls is covered in paintings and prints, and the themed rooms are decorated with antiques and many a theatrical flourish.

Halkin Hotel

5–6 Halkin Street, SW1; tel: 020-7333 1000; www.halkin.como.bz; tube: Hyde Park Corner; ££££

This modern five-star hotel, done out in a minimalist Italian aesthetic, is calm and cosseting, if a little on the impersonal side. Houses London's only Michelin-starred Thai restaurant.

The Rockwell

181 Cromwell Road, SW5; tel: 020-7244 2000; www.therockwellhotel.com; ££; tube: Earl's Court

Decorated in a contemporary homely style, the rooms feel cheerful and airy.

Vicarage Private Hotel

10 Vicarage Gate, W8; tel: 020-7229 4030; www.londonvicaragehotel.com; tube: Notting Hill Gate; £

Friendly place, with clean, simple rooms and good English breakfasts.

Price for a double room for one night without breakfast:

££££	over £300
£££	£200–300
££	£120–200
£	below £120

Bloomsbury and Holborn

Academy Hotel

21 Gower Street, WC1; tel: 020-7631 4115; www.theetoncollection.com; tube: Goodge Street; ££

A welcoming boutique hotel, situated in five interlinked townhouses. Comfortable rooms with traditional decor.

Charlotte Street Hotel

15–17 Charlotte Street, W1; tel: 020-7806 2000; www.firmdale.com; tube: Goodge Street; £££

This hotel successfully walks the line between old-fashioned quality and contemporary style, with soft colours and bold touches. There are mini-TVs in the marble bathrooms and there is a luxurious cinema in the basement. Art by members of the Bloomsbury set nods at the area's history.

Crescent Hotel

49–50 Cartwright Gardens, WC1; tel: 020-7387 1515; www.crescenthoteloflondon.com; tube: Russell Square, Euston; £

Simple but pleasant family-run hotel in a Georgian building on a quiet Bloomsbury crescent. Also has access to private gardens and tennis courts.

Hotel Russell

Russell Square, WC1; tel: 020-7837 6470; www.principal-hotels.com; tube: Russell Square; ££

This Victorian hotel, long a Bloomsbury landmark with its exuberantly baronial architecture, has recently undergone a £20-million refurbish-

ment. The public spaces are opulent, while the individually styled bedrooms are oases of calm in understated colours.

The City and East London
ANdAZ
40 Liverpool Street, EC2; tel: 020-7961 1234; www.london.liverpool street.andaz.com; tube: Liverpool Street; £££

A transformation of the Great Eastern Hotel, ANdAZ fits designer facilities into a venerable Victorian railway hotel. Rooms are simple and contemporary in style, if a little corporate.

Hoxton Hotel
81 Great Eastern Street, Old Street, EC2; tel: 020-7550 1000; www. hoxtonhotels.com; tube: Old Street; £

Innovative hotel with an urban funky look. The well-designed rooms offer excellent value. Watch the website for occasional offers of rooms for only £1.

Malmaison
Charterhouse Square, Clerkenwell, EC1; tel: 020-7012 3700; www. malmaison.com; tube: Barbican; £££

It is part of a chain, but the atmosphere and style for the price makes this a happy choice. In an attractive Victorian building, the hotel's rooms are comfortable and the brasserie dependable.

The Rookery
12 Peter's Lane, Cowcross Street, EC1; tel: 020-7336 0931; www.rookery hotel.com; tube: Farringdon; £££

The atmospheric Rookery features wood panelling, stone flagged floors, and open fires. The spacious bedrooms combine the historic with the contemporary: 18th-century beds, silk drapes, flat-screen TVs and wi-fi.

Threadneedles
5 Threadneedle Street, EC2; tel: 020-7657 8080; www.theeton collection.com; tube: Bank; ££

Located in a former bank building, Threadneedles blends modern comforts with Victorian splendour. There are even plasma TVs in the bathrooms.

Zetter Restaurant & Rooms
86–8 Clerkenwell Road, EC1; tel: 020-7324 4444; www.thezetter.com; tube: Farringdon; ££

At this quirky designer hotel set within a converted warehouse, champagne is dispensed from vending machines. Second-hand books and hot-water bottles are thoughtful extras in the chic but comfortable rooms.

South Bank and Bankside
Mad Hatter
3–7 Stamford Street, SE1; tel: 020-7401 9222; www.fullershotels.co.uk; tube: London Bridge, Southwark; ££

Large, colourful, contemporary-styled rooms above a Fullers pub, just a short stroll from Tate Modern.

Southwark Rose
47 Southwark Bridge Road, SE1; tel: 020-7015 1480; www.southwark rose hotel.co.uk; tube: London Bridge; ££

Sleek, simply designed hotel with clean, minimalist lines. Friendly staff.

Above from far left: grand exterior *(far left)* and guest room *(far right)* at ANdAZ, formerly the Great Eastern Hotel; guest room *(left)* and funky staircase *right)* at Zetter Restaurant & Rooms.

Facts and Figures
According to Visit London, the capital's tourist board, there are more than 100,000 rooms in the city as a whole, providing accommodation for over 27 million overnight visitors each year. This makes it the world's most popular city destination.

Alistair Little

49 Frith Street, W1; tel: 020-7734 5183; Mon–Fri L and D, Sat D only; tube: Leicester Square; £££–££££

Alistair Little's pioneering concept of modern European cooking has weathered the last 20 years well. Enjoy well cooked fresh produce in a light and stylish dining room.

Andrew Edmunds

46 Lexington Street, W1; tel: 020-7437 5708; daily L and D; tube: Piccadilly Circus; £££

A lack of signage gives an anonymous secretive feel to this romantic hideaway. Soft candlelight and wood panelling make it cosy and intimate. Dishes are simple but varied, ranging from beef to well-presented pasta. The staff are relaxed and friendly.

Café Emm

17 Frith Street, W1; tel: 020-7437 0723; daily L and D; tube: Leicester Square; £–££

Convivial and exceptionally good value, Café Emm is packed every night. The menu is conventional (fish cakes, lamb shank, fish and chips), but the food is very respectable and portions are large. Beware of queues and occasional boisterous birthday parties.

French House

49 Dean Street, W1; tel: 020-7437 2477; Mon–Sat L and D; tube: Leicester Square; £££

A Soho classic, mercifully little changed since its erstwhile *patron*, Victor Berlemont, passed on in 1999. The bustling pub downstairs serves beer only by the half pint (it was once a little too popular with famous sots such as Dylan Thomas and Francis Bacon). The cosy dining room upstairs serves comforting French classics.

The Ivy

1 West Street, WC2; tel: 020-7836 4751; daily L and D; tube: Covent Garden; £££–££££

Popular restaurant with celebrities, this is a place to see and be seen, and the food is a secondary consideration, though of decent quality (British classics plus international favourites). The downside is the difficulty in getting a table: reserve weeks, not days, ahead.

Mr Kong

21 Lisle Street, WC2; tel: 020-7437 7341; daily L and D; tube: Leicester Square; £–££

One of the more authentic Chinese restaurants in the area. Dishes include Kon Chi baby squid with chilli sauce or sandstorm crab. Vegetarian options.

Mildreds

45 Lexington Street, W1; tel: 020-

Price guide for an average two-course meal for one with a glass of wine:

££££	over £40
£££	£25–£40
££	£15–25
£	below £15

7494 1634; Mon–Sat L and D; tube: Piccadilly Circus; £

Sleek and stylish vegetarian restaurant which avoids the carrot casserole/nut bake stereotype. Instead feast on porcini and ale pie, Malaysian coconut curry, burritos, or ratatouille.

Rules

35 Maiden Lane, WC2; tel: 020-7836 5314; daily L and D; tube: Covent Garden; £££

Established in 1798, the decor reflects its heritage: floor-to-ceiling prints, gently revolving fans, chandeliers and red-velvet booths. The robust cuisine has stood the test of time with British ingredients of the highest quality: beef, lamb and game from Rules' own estate in the Pennines. Reservation advisable.

J Sheekey

28–32 St Martin's Court, WC2; tel: 020-7240 2565; daily L and D; tube: Leicester Square; £££–££££

Sister restaurant to The Ivy, J Sheekey is set in a series of panelled rooms hung with black-and-white theatre prints. It is a paradise for fish lovers: chargrilled squid with gorgonzola polenta, Cornish fish stew and New England baby lobster. Reserve.

Stockpot

18 Old Compton Street, W1; tel: 020-7287 1066; daily L and D; tube: Leicester Square; £

'The Pot' has been going for years, serving school-dinner-style food at extremely low prices. Also on the King's Road and Panton Street.

La Trouvaille

12a Newburgh St, W1; tel: 020-7287 8488; Mon–Sat L and D; tube: Oxford Circus; £££

Smart, intimate restaurant with a friendly atmosphere. Unobtrusive staff serve well-cooked, if sometimes unnecessarily elaborate, dishes with a French accent. High-quality ingredients.

Piccadilly, Mayfair and Marylebone

The Guinea Grill

30 Bruton Place, W1; tel: 020-7499 1210; Mon–Fri L and D, Sat D; tube: Oxford Circus, Green Park; £££

Old-world, wood-panelled pub-restaurant in a cobbled mews. Great steak and kidney pie, grills and oysters. Good choice of beers, wines and ports.

Greens Restaurant and Oyster Bar

36 Duke Street, SW1; tel: 020-7930 4566; daily L and D; tube: Bond Street; £££

Clubby St James's stalwart popular with the old school. Well-made traditional dishes include potted shrimps and lemon sole with perfect hollandaise. Excellent cheeseboard supplied by nearby Paxton & Whitfield.

Scotts

20 Mount Street, W1; tel: 020-7629 5248; daily L and D; tube: Marble Arch, Green Park; £££

This revamped institution continues to serve delicious fish dishes, including rarities such as stargazy pie. The old-fashioned puddings get a modern twist.

Above from far left: organic duck with lentils; the stylish RIBA café *(see p47)*; tempting cocktail; fish and chips.

Eating Out with Children
This need not be an ordeal. Although the maître d's face in many a smart restaurant may fall as you approach with a gaggle of tots in tow, there are at least some establishments that enjoy catering for children. Try Sticky Fingers (Phillimore Gardens), the children's restaurants in Harrods and Hamley's, or any of the cafés in London's parks. Look out also for branches of Giraffe (South Bank, Spitalfields Market, Brunswick Centre etc), and Carluccio's, which are usually very child-friendly.

Orrery

55 Marylebone High Street, W1; tel: 020-7616 8000; daily L and D; tube: Bond Street; £££

Barbary duck with pain d'épice, foie gras tarte Tatin and banyuls jus are typical of the intensely flavoured dishes at this elegant Conran restaurant. The wine list is good and the cheese trolley has won prizes.

Sketch

9 Conduit Street, W1; tel: 0870 777 44 88; Lecture Room Mon–Sat L and D, Gallery Mon–Sat D only; tube: Bond Street, Oxford Circus; ££££

The interior is decadently over-designed, and the food by Parisian super-chef Pierre Gagnaire is dizzily priced. Choose between the haute cuisine Lecture Room and the more informal Gallery, where, apparently, 'art meets food meets fashion'.

Criterion Grill

224 Piccadilly, W1; tel: 020-7930 0488; Mon–Sat L and D; tube: Piccadilly Circus; ££–£££

This newly revamped Marco Pierre White restaurant has a simple menu of French classics, all decently prepared. The opulent neo-Byzantine interior

---

Price guide for an average two-course meal for one with a glass of wine:

££££	over £40
£££	£25–£40
££	£15–25
£	below £15

---

is wonderful, and the pre-theatre set menu is very reasonably priced.

Kensington and Chelsea

Bibendum

Michelin House, 81 Fulham Road, SW3; tel: 020-7581 5817; daily L and D; tube: South Kensington; £££

Located in the proto-Art Deco Michelin building with its fine stained glass, chef Matthew Harris maintains high standards. Dishes such as grilled oysters with curried sauce and courgette linguine are faultless, the wine list is good and service excellent. Good-value lunchtime fixed-price menus. Reserve.

Cambio de Tercio

163 Old Brompton Road, SW5; tel: 020-7244 8970; daily L and D; tube: Gloucester Road; ££–£££

This bright, cheery little restaurant has won many accolades for its exciting food and impeccable service. Some think it is the best Spanish eaterie in town.

Chutney Mary

535 King's Road, SW10; tel: 020-7351 3113; Mon–Fri D only, Sat–Sun B and D; tube: Fulham Broadway; £££

First-class Indian restaurant with stylish decor and exceptional food. The chefs come from across the subcontinent, so take your pick of regional dishes.

Gordon Ramsay

68–9 Royal Hospital Road, SW3; tel: 020-7352 4441/3334; Mon–Fri L and D; tube: Sloane Square; ££££

The front is unobtrusive, the decor minimalist, the gastronomic experi-

ence impeccable. One of only three restaurants in Britain with three Michelin stars. Try such delights as fricassée of English snails with spinach, followed by chargrilled monkfish tail with crispy duck. The prices are very high so consider the excellent lunchtime set menu.

Papillon

96 Draycott Avenue, SW3; tel: 020-7225 2555; daily L and D; tube: South Kensington; £££

This French restaurant has a reconstructed ethic, offering vegetarian dishes alongside its French classics, and all served by friendly staff. It has 600 wines on its list and 20 are available by the glass. Good-value set lunch.

La Poule au Pot

231 Ebury Street SW1; tel: 020-7730 7763; daily L and D; tube: Sloane Square; ££–£££

This charming and romantic corner of France has occupied its Pimlico address for 30 years. Daily specials are decided as deliveries are made, and everything is very fresh and very French. Good-value set lunches.

Tom Aikens

43 Elystan Street, SW3; tel: 020-7584 2003; Mon–Fri L and D; tube: South Kensington; ££££

Michelin-starred modern French restaurant. Intensely flavoured dishes such as frogs' legs with poached lettuce, and pig's head braised with spices and ginger demonstrate Aikens' culinary craftsmanship and flair.

Bloomsbury and Fitzrovia

Fryer's Delight

19 Theobald's Road, WC1; tel: 020-7405 4114; Mon–Sat noon–10pm; tube: Holborn; £

One of the few remaining fish and chip shops in central London.

Leith's

113 Chancery Lane, WC2; tel: 020-7316 5580; Mon–Fri L (snack menu 5–9pm); tube: Chancery Lane; ££

An offshoot of Leith's Cookery School, this relaxed place is ideal for a light, fresh lunch. Its eclectic menu may include citrus-crusted lamb rump alongside spinach and blue cheese gnocchi, and seafood risotto. Reserve.

Pied à Terre

34 Charlotte Street, W1; tel: 020-7636 1178; Mon–Fri L and D, Sat D only; tube: Goodge Street; ££££

Fitzrovia's most prestigious restaurant has now regained its second Michelin star, under Australian chef Shane Osborn. The eight-course tasting menu is £80, but the set lunch is a bargain.

The City

Clark's

46 Exmouth Market, EC1; tel: 020-7837 1974; Mon–Sat, all day; tube: Farringdon; £

One of London's few remaining pie-and-mash shops standing its ground among the fast-food chains. The worn wooden pews, tiled floors, low prices and no-nonsense service keep this excellent tradition alive. Cash only.

Above from far left: Sketch; invitation to the bar; home-made ice cream at the Seven Stars (see p.54); petals at the Cinammon Club (see p.27).

Tipping
In Britain, it is customary to add 10 per cent on to the bill for service. Be careful, though, that you do not pay for service twice, since some restaurants add this (or sometimes even more – up to 15 per cent) to the bill automatically. Of course, if you are less than satisfied with the service received, do not hesitate to leave a smaller tip, or none at all. You might also check with the waiting staff whether they get to keep the tips themselves or whether the management pockets them instead.

Coach & Horses

26–8 Ray Street, EC1; tel: 020-7657 8088; Mon–Fri L and D, Sat D only, Sun L only; tube: Farringdon; ££

Of the many gastropubs trying to make their mark across the city, this is one of the best. The scrubbed-wood decor is simple but homely, the food inventive but unpretentious, the wines well priced and the service good-natured.

The Eagle

159 Farringdon Road, EC1; tel: 020-7837 1353; Mon–Sat L and D, Sun L only; tube: Farringdon; ££

Pub serving reasonable food with a Mediterranean bias, complemented by an extensive range of European beers. Gets crowded quickly, so arrive early.

Moro

34–6 Exmouth Market, EC1; tel: 020-7833 8336; Mon–Fri L and D, Sat D only; tube: Farringdon; ££

The excellent food on Moro's lively Spanish–North African menu includes charcoal grilled lamb and wood-roasted pork. Friendly service.

The Quality Chop House

94 Farringdon Road, EC1; tel: 020-7837 5093; Mon–Fri B, Sun–Fri L and D, Sat D only; tube: Farringdon; ££

It is the nostalgic setting that recommends this restored Victorian cafe – the food (traditional British) is average.

Rudland & Stubbs

35–7 Greenhill's Rents, Cowcross Street, EC1; tel: 020-7253 0148; Mon–Fri L and D; tube: Farringdon; ££

This attractive fish restaurant in a converted sausage factory does a brisk lunchtime trade. It prides itself on the freshness of the fish served in unfussy dishes such as tuna niçoise, crab Caesar salad, and of course fish and chips.

St John

26 St John Street, EC1; tel: 020-7251 0848; Mon–Fri L and D, Sat D only; tube: Farringdon; £££

A stone's throw from Smithfield meat market, this restaurant is stark but elegant. In the main dining room, the meat- and offal-heavy menu changes with the season. Chef Fergus Henderson's signature roast bone-marrow and parsley salad is always on the menu, and whole roast suckling pig may make an appearance.

Smiths of Smithfield

66–67 Charterhouse Street, EC1; tel: 020-7251 7950; daily B, L and D; ££ (brunch); tube: Farringdon; ££–£££

Brunch on a Saturday or Sunday is great fun in this buzzing post-industrial complex. Tuck into a cooked breakfast, grilled minute steak, or corned beef hash. The restaurant upstairs is more refined and more expensive.

The South Bank

The Anchor and Hope

36 The Cut, SE1; tel: 020-7928 9898; daily L and D; tube: Waterloo; ££

Inspired by St John *(see above)*, all the produce here is British, and the meat – featured strongly on the menu – is butchered on the premises. Try perfectly cooked roast neck of lamb with

ratatouille. Keen prices, hefty portions and friendly staff.

Mesón Don Felipe

53 The Cut, SE1; tel: 020-7928 3237; Mon–Sat L and D, Sun D only; tube: Waterloo; ££

A busy little place with a great atmosphere and lots of tasty tapas. The drinks list is an education in Spanish wines. Bookings taken before 8pm; after that it is first come first served.

East London

Fifteen

15 Westland Place, N1; tel: 0871-330 1515; daily B, L and D; tube: Old Street; £££

Run by Jamie Oliver, every year this restaurant apprentices disadvantaged young people into its kitchen and tries to transform them into Italian chefs that even The River Café would be proud of. Even if, though, the dishes are not always perfectly executed, it is fascinating to see this project in action.

The Real Greek & Mezedopolio

14–15 Hoxton Market, N1; tel: 020-7739 8212; Mon–Sat L and D; tube: Old Street; ££

Mezze regulars are moussakas, tiny shellfish and tomato cutlets. Main courses include stocky lamb or beef pasta dishes, and there are distinctive cheeses and pastries. Not what it used to be, but still well worth a visit.

Story Deli

3 Dray Walk, The Old Truman Brewery, 91 Brick Lane, E1; tel: 020-7247 3137; daily B, L and D; tube: Liverpool Street; £

This entirely organic pizzeria is easily missed from the street, but it is worth taking some time to find it, not only for its outstanding pizzas, but also for its tasty kebabs, sandwiches, scrumptious cakes and coffee.

West London

Lisboa Pâtisserie

57 Golborne Road, W10; tel: 020-8968 5242; daily 8am–7.30pm; tube: Westbourne Park; £

In the bustle of this cafe's tiled interior, take a café galao and pastel de nata.

The River Café

Thames Wharf, Rainville Road, W6; tel: 020-7386 4200; Mon–Sat L and D; tube: Hammersmith; £££–££££

The River Café is a west London institution, and its international reputation for fine Italian food is well deserved (as is its reputation for high prices). Only the best produce is selected by the owners, Ruth Rogers and Rose Gray. Dishes such as char-grilled scallops with deep-fried artichokes, beef with tomatoes and spinach are faultless. Booking some time ahead is essential.

Above from far left: Regent's Park's Honest Sausage (see p.47); mallards' legs at St John; daily specials on the blackboard; one of the capital's many trendy restaurants.

School Puddings Many British people retain a particular fondness for the traditional puddings of their schooldays. These include spotted dick, treacle sponge pudding, jam roly poly, trifle, bread-and-butter pudding, sticky toffee pudding, apple Charlotte, rhubarb crumble and rice pudding. Many of the above are considerably enhanced with a good dollop of custard. Children's author Enid Nesbit summed up the peculiar satisfaction of one such pudding as follows: 'Jam roly gives you a peaceful feeling and you do not at first care if you never play any runabout game ever any more.'

CREDITS

Insight Step by Step London
Written by: Michael Macaroon
Series Editor: Clare Peel
Cartography: James Macdonald/Zoë Goodwin
Picture Managers: Hilary Genin/Steven Lawrence
Photography by: Apa: Natasha Babaian, David Beatty, Jay Fechtman, Glyn Genin, Tony Halliday, Britta Jaschinski, Sian Lezard, Michael Macaroon, Clare Peel, Dorothy Stannard, Sarah Sweeney except: AKG 44TR; Alamy 8/9, 12TR, 13TL, 13BR, 22/3, 49T, 72T, 73T, 82TL, 84T, 86T, 87T, 90TL, 91TL, 94T, 100/1; ANdaZ/Hyatt 116TL, 116TR; William Beckett 28C; Bridgeman Art Library 31T, 32TL, 32BL, 76TR, 77TR, 207TR; Brown's Hotel 112TL, 112TR; Cadogan Hotel 114TR, 115TL; Julian Calder 53TR; Corbis 34T, 35T, 44TL, 47TR, 48T, 71TL, 74TL, 81T, 92TL; Duke's Hotel 113TR; Geffrye Museum 92B; Getty 11CBR; Halkin Hotel 114TL; Courtesy Harrods 19BR, 80BL; Indexstock/ Photolibrary 67TR; Lebrecht Music 63BR; Pavel Libera 10TL; Alisdair Macdonald 20/1T, 47TL, 103, 104, 105, 108, 109, 111; James Macdonald 37BR; Courtesy Madame Tussauds 45B; National Portrait Gallery/ ©Michael Seymour 33TR; National Portrait Gallery 33TL; ©RBG Kew 6BR, 98TL, 98TR, 99TL, 99TR, 99B; Science & Society Picture Library 79BR; Soho Hotel 113TL; SuperStock 55T; ©Tate 70TL; ©Tate. Photo: Andy Paradise 68TL; ©Tate London 2004 71TR; ©Tate 2007 70CL; Courtesy of Visit London 10TR, 11TR, 12TL, 24TL, 24TR, 26TL, 30T, 32TR, 35CR, 39TR, 39BR, 40TL, 41TL, 55BR, 64BL, 69TL, 77TL, 80T, 80CL, 82TR, 89TR, 93TR; Adam Woolfitt/Robert Harding 10BL, 14TL; V&A 77BR; Zetter 117TL, 117TR.
Front Cover: Alamy; SuperStock; Istockphoto.
Printed by: Insight Print Services (Pte) Ltd, 38 Joo Koon Road, Singapore 628990.

Maps reproduced by permission of Geographers' A–Z Map Co. Ltd. Licence No. B4290. Crown Copyright 2008. All rights reserved. Licence number 100017302.

DISTRIBUTION

Worldwide
Apa Publications GmbH & Co. Verlag KG (Singapore branch)
38 Joo Koon Road, Singapore 628990
Tel: (65) 6865 1600. Fax: (65) 6861 6438

UK and Ireland
GeoCenter International Ltd
Meridian House, Churchill Way West, Basingstoke, Hampshire, RG21 6YR
Tel: (44) 01256 817 987. Fax: (44) 01256 817 988

United States
Langenscheidt Publishers, Inc.
36–36 33rd Street, 4th Floor, Long Island City, NY 11106
Tel: (1) 718 784 0055. Fax: (1) 718 784 0640

Australia
Universal Publishers
1 Waterloo Road, Macquarie Park, NSW 2113
Tel: (61) 2 9857 3700. Fax: (61) 2 9888 9074

New Zealand
Hema Maps New Zealand Ltd (HNZ)
Unit D, 24 Ra ORA Drive, East Tamaki, Auckland
Tel: (64) 9 273 6459. Fax: (64) 9 273 6479

CONTACTING THE EDITORS

We would appreciate it if readers would alert us to errors or outdated information by writing to us at insight@apaguide.co.uk or Apa Publications, PO Box 7910, London SE1 1WE, UK.

www.insightguides.com

INDEX

A

accommodation 112–7
Adam, Robert 72
Admiralty Arch 29
airports 102
    accommodation 113
Albany, The 41
Albert Memorial 75
All Hallow's Church 84
antiques 18, 19, 89
Apsley House 72
Arcola Theatre 93

B

banks 107–8
Bank of England 54, 56
Banqueting House 26
Barbican 59
Barfield, Julia 61, 70
Barry, Sir Charles 25, 27
Bart's (hospital) 59
BBC 41
beer 16
Big Ben 27
Billingsgate Market 17, 56
Blair, Tony 21, 53
Blake, William 41
Bloomsbury 48–51
blue plaques 107
boating 47, 74
boat cruises 110
Bond Street 43
Boudicca 20
Bow Street Runners 35
bowling 51
Borough Market 17, 66–7
brass rubbing 26
Brick Lane 91–2
Brief Encounter 47
British Museum 48–50
British Film Institute 62–3
Brompton Oratory 80
Brook Street 43

Brown, Gordon 21
Brunswick Centre 51
Buckingham Palace 29, 30
Burgh House 87
Burlington Arcade 42
Burton, Decimus 46, 73, 98, 99
buses 109–10

C

Cabinet War Rooms 29
Canary Wharf 93
Carlton House Terrace 29
Carlyle, Thomas 50, 83
Carlyle's House 83
carnival 89
Cartoon Museum 50
Cavalry, Household 73
Central St Martin's School of Art 50
Chancery Lane 54
Changing the Guard 26, 30
Channel Tunnel 102
Charles, Prince 30, 31
Charlie Wright's International Bar 93
Charing Cross Road 37
Chaucer, Geoffrey 28
Chelsea 81–3
Chelsea Flower Show 82
Chelsea Old Church 83
Chelsea Physic Garden 83
Chester Gate 46
Cheyne Walk 83
children 103, 119
Chinatown 39
Christchuch Spitalfields 91
Christmas tree 24
Churchill, Sir Winston 28, 31, 67
cider 17
cinema 39, 51, 54, 62–3, 89, 92
City, The 55–59
Civil War 20

Clarence House 29
Claridge's 43, 113
classical concerts 44, 45, 62, 66, 75
Clink Street Museum 65
climate 12, 103
Clockmakers' Museum 57
College of Arms 57
Columbia Road (Flower) Market 92, 93
congestion charge 21, 104
Coram's Fields 50
Cork Street 42
Courtauld Gallery 54
Covent Garden 34–7
County Hall 60–1
Coward, Noel 37, 43, 80
crime 103
Crystal Palace 73, 76
currency 107–8
Custom House 56
customs regulations 103
Cutty Sark 94–5
cycling 104

D

Dalí Universe 61
Denmark Street 37
Dennis Severs' House 91
Diana, Princess of Wales 74, 75
Diana, Princess of Wales Memorial Playground 75
Dickens, Charles 37, 50, 52, 54, 67, 88, 95
Dickens Museum 50
Diorama 46
disabled access 104
Docklands 93
Docklands Light Railway 109
Docklands Museum 93
Donmar Warehouse 35
Downing Street 26
Dr Johnson's House 53
Dracula 40

Drake, Sir Francis 66
driving 104
Duke of York Square 82

E

East End 91
East London Mosque 91
electricity 105
Elgin Marbles 49
embassies 105
emergencies 105
English National Opera 37
Eros 41
ethnicity 10–11
Eurostar 102
Egyptian antiquities 49, 51

F

Fan Museum 96
Fenton House 86–7
Fire, the Great 20, 85
Fleet Street 52–3, 85
food and drink 14–17, 118–23
Foreign Office, the 26
Fortnum and Mason 42
Foster, Norman 49, 58, 64, 84
Foundling Museum 50–1
Freud, Sigmund 86
Freud Museum 86
Frith Street 38
frost fairs 12, 62

G

Gabriel's Wharf 64
gay and lesbian 106
Geffrye Museum 93
geography 12–13
Gerrard Street 39
Gherkin, The 58, 84
Gibbons, Grinling 25, 41
Gilbert Collection 54
Gipsy Moth IV 95
Gladstone, W. E. 26, 41, 95
Globe Theatre 20, 21, 64–5
Golden Hinde, The 65–6

Goldfinger, Erno 87, 89
gorillas 47
Great Exhibition 21, 73, 74, 76
Greek Street 38
Greenwich 94–7
Guards Museum 29
Guildhall and art gallery 57
Guy Fawkes and the Gun-
    powder Plot 20, 27, 55
Gywnn, Nell 26, 35

H

Hendrix, Jimi 37, 39, 43
Hamley's 41
Hampstead 86–7
Hampton Court 99
Handel, George Frederick
    36, 43, 51
Handel House Museum 43
Harley Street 44
Harrods 80
Harvard, John 66
Harvey Nichols 80
Hawksmoor, Nicholas
    28, 50, 56, 75
Hay's Galleria 67
Hayward Gallery 62
Hazlitt, William 38
health 106
history 20–1
HMS Belfast 67
Hogarth, William 26, 51, 54, 59
Holborn 52–4
Horse Guards 26
horse riding 75
hotels 112–7
Hoxton 92–3
Huguenots 11, 39, 91, 93
Hunterian Museum 54
Hyde Park 72–5

I

ICA (Institute of
    Contemporary Arts) 29
Inns of Court 53–54
internet 106

J

Jack the Ripper 67, 91
jazz 39, 62, 93
Jermyn Street 41
Johnson, Samuel 13, 53, 67, 83
Jones, Inigo 26, 29, 35,
    36, 37, 96

K

karaoke 39
Keats, John 87
Keats House 87
Kensington Gardens 72, 74–5
Kensington Palace 75
Kenwood House 87
Kew Bridge Steam Museum
    98
Kew Gardens 12, 98–9
Kew Palace 99
Knightsbridge 80

L

Lamb's Conduit Street
Landseer, Edwin 25, 57
Lasdun, Denys 46
left luggage 106
Leicester Square 39
Liberty & Co 41
Lincoln's Inn Fields 54
Livingstone, Ken 21
London Aquarium 61
London Bridge 12, 56
London Dungeon 67
London Eye 61
London Imax 63
London Transport Museum
    36–7
lost property 106
Lutyens, Edwin 25, 26

M

Mall, the 28–9
Mansion House 56
maps 107

markets **17, 19, 36, 59, 66, 89, 91, 92, 97**
Marks, David **61, 70**
Marlborough House **29**
Marylebone **44–5**
mayor **12, 21**
Mayfair **42–3**
media **107**
medical care **106**
Meridian (Greenwich) **97**
Michelin stars **14**
Millenium Dome **95**
Millenium Bridge **64**
money **107**
Monument, The **56, 85**
Mozart, Wolfgang Amadeus **38**
Mudchute City Farm **93**
Museum of London **59**
Museum of the Bank of England **56**

N

Namco Station **61**
Napoleon **18, 25, 72**
Nash, John **28, 29, 30, 41, 46**
National Army Museum **82**
National Gallery **25, 31–3**
Natural History Museum **78–9**
National Maritime Museum **95**
National Portrait Gallery **33**
National Theatre **63**
NatWest Tower **56, 58, 85**
Neal Street **35**
Nelson, Admiral Lord **25, 58, 95–6**
newspapers **107**
Notting Hill **88–9**

O

Old Bailey **85**
Old Compton Street **39**
Old Curiosity Shop **54**
Old Royal Observatory **97**

Old Truman Brewery **92**
Olympics **11, 21, 90**
Orwell, George **51, 72, 86, 89**
Oyster cards **109–10**
Oxford Street **43**
OXO Tower **63**

P

Pall Mall **29**
Pankhurst, Emmeline **32**
Paolozzi, Edoardo **48**
parks and gardens **46–7, 50, 58, 72–5, 82, 87, 97, 98–9**
Parliament, Houses of **26-7**
Pepys, Samuel **36, 67, 72**
Percival David Foundation of Chinese Art **51**
Petrie Museum of Egyptian Archaeology **51**
Peter Pan **75**
Petticoat Lane **91**
Photographer's Gallery **37**
Piccadilly **40–42**
Planetarium **97**
Poets' Corner **28**
politics **12**
population **10–11**
Port of London Authority **84**
Portobello Road **88–9**
postal services **108**
postcodes **108**
Postman's Park **58**
Princess Diana Memorial Fountain **74**
public holidays **108–9**
public transport **109–10**
Pudding Lane **56, 85**
Pugin, A.W. **27**
Purcell Room **62**

Q

Queen's Chapel **29**
Queen Elizabeth Hall **62**
Queen's Gallery **30**
Queen's House (Greenwich) **97**

R

Raleigh, Sir Walter **28, 55**
Ramsay, Gordon **14, 43, 113, 120–1**
Ranger's House **97**
Regent Street **41**
Regent's Park **46–7**
Rennie, John **56, 74**
restaurants **118–23**
Reynolds, Joshua **26, 42, 51**
Rich Mix (cinema, gallery) **92**
Rivington Place (gallery) **92**
Ronnie Scott's **39**
Routemaster bus **84–5**
Rose Exhibition (theatre) **65**
Royal Academy of Arts **42**
Royal Academy of Music **45**
Royal Albert Hall **75**
Royal Botanic Gardens **98–9**
Royal College of Physicians **46**
Royal Court Theatre **81**
Royal Courts of Justice **54**
Royal Exchange **56**
Royal Festival Hall **62**
Royal Hospital Chelsea **82**
Royal Mews **30**
Royal Naval College **95**
Royal Opera House **35–6**

S

Saatchi Gallery **82**
St Alfege **94**
St Anne and St Agnes **58**
St Bartholomew-the-Great **59**
St Bartholomew-the-Less **59**
St Botolph-Without-Aldersgate **58**
St Bride's **52, 85**
St Christopher's Place **44**
St Clement Danes **54, 85**
St Clement Eastcheap **56**
St Dunstan-in-the-West **53**
St James's Park **28**

St James's Palace **29**
St James Piccadilly **41**
St George's Hanover Square **43**
St George's Bloomsbury **50**
St John's, Hampstead **86**
St Katherine's Dock **55**
St Magnus the Martyr **56**
St Margaret's **28**
St Margaret Pattens **85**
St Martin-in-the-Fields **25**
St Martin's **85**
St Mary-le-Bow **57**
St Mary-le-Strand **85**
St Mary Woolnoth **56**
St Marylebone **45**
St Paul's Cathedral **57–8, 85**
St Paul's Covent Garden **37**
St Stephen Walbrook **56, 85**
St Vedast **57**
Savile Row **42**
Savoy Hotel **85, 112**
Science Museum **79–80**
Scott, George Gilbert **26, 74**
Scott, Giles Gilbert **27, 68**
Selfridges **43**
Senate House Library **51**
Serpentine **73**
Serpentine Gallery **74**
Seven Dials **35**
Shakespeare, William **20, 21, 33, 64–5**
Shakespeare's Globe **64–5**
Shelley, Percy Bysshe **13, 49, 73**
Shepherd Market **43**
Sherlock Holmes **45**
shopping **18–19**
Shoreditch **92–3**
Silver Vaults, the London **54**
Sir John Soane's Museum **54**
skating, ice **12, 54, 74**
Sloane Square **81**

Smithfield Market **59**
smoking **110**
Soane, Sir John **54, 56**
Soho **38–9**
Somerset House **54, 85**
Sotheby's **43**
South Kensington **76–80**
Southbank **60–7**
Southbank Centre **61**
Southwark Cathedral **66**
Speakers' Corner **72**
Spitalfields **91**
sport **11**
Stock Exchange, London **57**
student travellers **110**
Sweeney Todd **53, 67**

T

Tate Britain **70–1**
Tate Modern **64, 68–9**
taxis **11, 110**
telephones **110–11**
Temple Bar **54, 85**
Thatcher, Margaret **61, 83**
theatre **35, 41, 47, 63, 64–5, 81, 93**
Thornhill, Sir James **58, 96**
time **111**
tipping **121**
toilets **111**
tour operators **111**
tourist offices **111**
Tower Bridge **55, 67**
Tower of London **55**
Trafalgar Square **24, 85**
trains **102–3, 109**
Trellick Tower **89**
tube (London Underground) **21, 37, 109**
Turner Prize **70**
Turner, J.M.W. **71, 83**
Turpin, Dick **87**
Tussauds, Madame **45, 80**

U

Underground, the London
see tube
United Nations **27**
University of London **51**

V

Vanburgh's House **97**
Victoria and Albert Museum (V&A) **76–8**
Victoria Memorial **29**
Vinopolis **65**
Vortex Jazz Club **93**

W

Wallace Collection **44–5**
Washington, George **25**
Waterloo Sunset Pavilion **62**
websites **111**
weights and measures **111**
Wellington, Duke of **58, 72**
Westminster Abbey **27**
Westwood, Vivienne **81**
whisky **17**
Whitehall **26**
White Cube (gallery) **93**
Whitechapel Art Gallery **90–1**
Wigmore Hall **44**
Wilde, Oscar **35**
Willow Road, no.2 **87**
wine **16–17**
Winston Churchill's Britain at War Museum **67**
Whittington, Dick **57**
Women's Library **90**
Wren, Sir Christopher **57–8**

Z

Zoo, London **47**